MARY · EMMERLING'S
AMERICAN COUNTRY
WEST

MARY · EMMERLING'S AMERICAN COUNTRY WEST

PHOTOGRAPHS BY MICHAEL SKOTT
DESIGN BY RICHARD TRASK
TEXT BY CAROL SAMA SHEEHAN

Clarkson N. Potter, Inc./Publishers

TO MY FATHER, JULIAN G. ELLISOR, JR.
1919–1984

TO THE HARRISON FAMILY
RICH IN HISTORY

Other photographs, not already credited, by Chris Mead: page viii: bottom center, bottom right; page ix: top right; page 17: top left, center far right, bottom left, bottom right; page 21: top left and top center; pages 24-25: top left, top center, top right, above left, above center, below left, below center, bottom left, bottom center; page 29: top far right; pages 30-31: top center right, center right, bottom left, bottom center, bottom right; page 34: center right; page 35: center; pages 246-247: top left, center top left, center top right, center left, bottom far left, bottom left, bottom center left, bottom right. Other photo-

graph by Dick Rowan: page 35: bottom center.

Unless a particular photograph is indicated by an arrow, all photographs on facing pages are by the photographer whose credit appears.

Copyright ©1985 by Mary Ellisor Emmerling
Photographs copyright © 1985 by Michael Skott

Published by Clarkson N. Potter, Inc., 201 East 50th Street, New York, New York 10022.
Member of the Crown Publishing Group. Random House, Inc. New York, Toronto, London, Sydney, Auckland.

CLARKSON N. POTTER, POTTER, and colophon are trademarks of Clarkson N. Potter, Inc.

Manufactured in Singapore

Library of Congress Cataloging-in-Publication Data

Emmerling, Mary Ellisor.
   Mary Emmerling's American country West

   Includes index.

   1. Folk art—West (U.S.)
   2. Decoration and ornament—West (U.S.)   3. Indians of North America—West (U.S.)—Art.   I. Sheehan, Carol Sama.   II. Title
   III.Title:American country West.

NK823.E45 1985   745'.097884-26451
ISBN 0-517-88140-3

10 9 8 7 6 5 4 3 2 1

First Paperback Edition

ACKNOWLEDGMENTS

American Country West has been a very happy trail of discovering new places, making new friends, and visiting old friends.

The book has its roots in my family history, which mixed politics and pioneering spirit. An uncle, William H. Harrison, Jr., a congressman from Wyoming, was always talking about the ranch back home, and, for me, the West became a romance and mystery I wanted to see for myself. I owe my Uncle Bill and Aunt Betty a special thanks.

The idea of actually undertaking a book on the West came to me after my first trip to Texas, when I met Beverly and Tommy Jacomini. During evenings at his restaurant, the Hofbrau, Tommy regaled me with stories of the region. The Jacominis took me to Gilley's, introduced me to cowboy hats and boots, and let us photograph their farmhouse, a true Texas original.

There are a few other special friends who provided a hitch up into the saddle: Nancy Reynolds, whose spectacular log cabin appears in the book, and whose favorite western memories are the subject of its cover; Gloria List, whose store, Nonesuch, in Santa Monica, California, is where I started collecting western antiques, and who showed us some great houses; Buffy Birrittella, at Ralph Lauren, who was so helpful in finding locations and led us to Sundance, Utah; Cheri Carter, who never stops being a generous friend, and always introduces us to more country friends; Elaine Horwitch, whose galleries in Scottsdale, Arizona, and Santa Fe, New Mexico, inspired us, and who took us to so many exquisite homes, including her own.

I am also grateful to some places and people who were my sources and inspirations: the Wyoming Tourist Commission and the Cheyenne Rodeo, "the Daddy of 'em all"; the friends in Sheridan, Wyoming, that my aunt, Betty Harrison, introduced us to, especially Eaton's Dude Ranch and the Mint Bar; Oakleigh Thorne II and the Valley Ranch where I rode a horse again; Jane, Marshall, and Lee Dominick and the Seven D Ranch; Yellowstone National Park and Old Faithful—the best!; Paul Fees at the Buffalo Bill Historical Center in Cody, Wyoming; Bob Edgar of Old Trail Town, one of the most perfect restorations I have ever seen; Claire Radford and Varue Gordon of the Pico Adobe Museum; at Sundance Ski Area, special thanks to Brent Beck, Debbie Thalman, and Ed Johnson; and to all the mountain men who love the West.

This book could never have been written without the craftsmen and homeowners whose sense of style and western spirit infuse every page. My thanks to: Bill Bell who keeps me looking western with his belts; Bill Brown and Jim Josoff; MacDonald Becket; Dean Beaudet; Steve and Chris Cappellucci; Ryan Carey and Mac McLean of Artefacts; Lee and Robbie Cochran; Robert and Jackie Caywood, who shared so many western stories with us; Ken Dudwick and Paul Drymalski, who have a western cabin that is pure heaven; Hart and T. K. Empie; Clint Fay; Mr. and Mrs. Alexander Girard, who gave their wonderful collection to the Museum of Folk Art of Santa Fe; Skip Glomb; Barbara Gray, who introduced us to Al Luevand; Priscilla Hoback and Peter Gould, who always open their doors to us, no matter how busy they are; "Slim" Green, who had the best rodeo stories and tales of the West;

Mac Grimmer; Stan and Melody Hopper; Mrs. Lyndon B. Johnson; Betty Tilson; Mr. and Mrs. Kulhman; King's Saddlery; Andy Hysong; Ruth Ann Montgomery; Rosalea Murphy, who owns the Pink Adobe, the best place to eat in Santa Fe; Dr. Alan Minge; Frank Magleby; John and Renee Nieto, who made me stop and appreciate the special moments in life; Bob Nelson; David Ortega; Fred Pottinger and Tom Messer; Sydney and Claire Pollack; Jackie Peralta-Ramos; Ann Sams; Mrs. Eric Sloane and the late Eric Sloane; Jacobo, Isabelle, and Irvin Trujillo; Bruce Weber and Nan Bush.

My appreciation always to my friends and colleagues in New York: Jody Greif, who helps me coming and going. I couldn't do any of this without her organization, support, and kindness. Carol Sama Sheehan, whose expert writing made this the smoothest and best book we have done, and who is a joy, every day, to work with. Richard Trask, whose design and details bring the book to life.

And to the photographers: Michael Skott, who finds me hearts, for his dedication and his remarkably beautiful pictures; Chris Mead, who takes exquisite pictures for all the books, and always cares; Dick Rowan, who helped us get those western photos that required being there twenty-four hours a day.

And to all my new friends: at Springs Industries, Christine Corso, Dave Kaliski, and Beth Carrington; at J. C. Penney, Pat Starr, Maggie Phillips, and many others; at Hallmark Cards, Mary Ann Odom, Roger Emley, Bet David, Kathy Hutchinson, Martha Nagley, and Fred Klemushin; and all their inspiration to keep Country going.

I continue to be indebted to Gayle Benderoff and Deborah Geltman, my dedicated and wise agents, and to all my friends and supporters at Clarkson N. Potter and Crown Publishers, Inc.: Nancy Novogrod, who is the best editor in the whole world (I should know after three books); Carol Southern, to whom I feel a special closeness after the tough year we have been through together; Michael Fragnito, a special supporter; Nat Wartels, chairman of Crown Publishers, who knows that Country is forever; Lynne Arany, for all her helpful efforts; Gael Towey Dillon, who has an eye for design and a sense of order; Laurie Stark, Ann Cahn, and Teresa Nicholas for the production; Michelle Sidrane, Phyllis Fleiss, and Jo Fagan in subsidiary rights; Nancy Kahan, Barbara Marks, and Susan Butler in publicity, who keep me on the road long after the book is finished; Gail Shanks in sales; and always to the Crown Publishers sales force who make the books bestsellers.

First and always, my love and appreciation go out to Samantha and Jonathan, who let me travel and bring them back all the wonderful stories that will be their heritage; to my mother, Marthena Ellisor, who has given me my heritage, along with never-ending warmth and love; to Juanita Jones, now ten years with us—Jonathan, Samantha, and me; and to Terry, the best brother ever.

And, always, to "Smokey The Bear" who helps us preserve the West.

Happy Trails to You . . .
Until We Meet Again.

Mary Emmerling

October 1984

CONTENTS

Introduction/1

1 This Is American Country West/5

2 Homes of the West/37

3 West in the East/173

4 Cowboy and Indian Crafts/197

5 Western Heritage: People, Places, and Events/233

Directory of Stores, Galleries, and Craftsmen/255

Directory of Museums and Historic Sites/268

Index/277

INTRODUCTION

Although I spent some of my early years in Minot, North Dakota, most of my first impressions of the West came, not from my immediate world, but from Gene Autry, Roy Rogers, Hopalong Cassidy, and other cowboy heroes. Like many American children of my era, I passed untold numbers of Saturday afternoons watching these white knights in western gear ride roughshod over their foes.

Apart from absorbing the Hollywood interpretations of frontier life, I had reason to take a personal interest in the historical American West. My great-great-great-great grandfather,

NATIVE AMERICANS (*left*), today more than ever, are recognized for their distinctive contributions to our way of life. Indian arts, customs, and traditions are an integral part of western culture.

AMERICAN PRESIDENTS William Henry Harrison and Benjamin Harrison (*above*) are part of the Emmerling family line.

William Henry Harrison, was the ninth president of the United States. Though he only served in office briefly—he died 31 days after his inauguration—he was the man who, as Secretary of the Northwest Territories, negotiated the numerous Indian treaties that opened the way to American settlement of much of our uncharted land. My great-great grandfather was Benjamin Harrison, president of the United States from 1889 to 1893. During his term of office, six western states—North Dakota, South Dakota, Montana, Washington, Idaho, and Wyoming —all were admitted to the Union.

But, even with this personal heritage, it wasn't until I began traveling throughout the West, gathering material

COWBOY CLOTHING AND EQUIPMENT (*this page and following pages*), collected by Californian A. V. Luevand, include the essentials for life on the range.

for the books *American Country* and *Collecting American Country* that I came to appreciate and understand the western legacy all Americans share.

As I moved from place to place within the region, I was struck first by the scale and variety of the land itself. I remember driving for hours across the seemingly endless monochro-

matic terrain of New Mexico, then suddenly coming upon Santa Fe with all its brilliant Indian colors. When I drove through Colorado, it was spring. The river was full from winter run-off and the land was green and lush. Not just the mountains, everything in Colorado appears bigger and bolder. Wyoming's monumental landscape almost looked artificial to me, as though huge, theatrical backdrops had been painted along the horizon. Here you can see for miles and miles and even tall buildings are dwarfed by the big sky.

The more time I spent in the region, the more I discovered that western-ers have their own way of doing things that affects their homes, their friendships, how they conduct business, how they entertain—every aspect of life. It's a dis-tinctive living style and philosophy underscored by the virtues of honesty, integrity, and respect for tradition.

If the heart of the American West is the land, then its soul is surely the people. For the past 15 years, A. V. Luevand, a westerner who grew up in awe of the authentic working cowboy, has been assem-

People like A. V. Luevand, Slim Green, and the Edgars, who care so deeply about who and what came before them, are our true westerners. Their commitment to keep the West in place—in the houses they inhabit, the customs they practice, and the heritage they honor and preserve—has made this book, *American Country West,* possible.

bling what may be the ultimate personal homage to the early western buckaroo. Luevand's collection of cowboy gear, chaps, vests, hats, belts, and weapons is not only of interest to collectors and amateur western buffs, but, as an archive of the life and times of an enduring American folk character, to scholars of the American West as well.

Stepping into saddle-

maker Slim Green's Tesuque, New Mexico, workshop is like journeying back into the days of the frontier. The smells, the tools, and the saddles-in-progress are proof that old cowboys never die, they just keep passing down their trade and their traditions.

For me, Wyoming native Bob Edgar is the epitome of dedication to preserving the western ideal. A painter, amateur

19th-century historian, and self-taught sharpshooter, Edgar and his wife Terry made numerous personal sacrifices to save a part of the West that was important to them. They rescued a group of early buildings from oblivion by moving them from their original sites to Trail Town, their Wyoming restoration, and returning them to the condition of their glory days on the frontier.

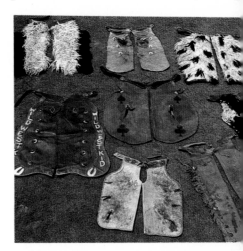

1

This Is American Country West

This is American Country WEST

American Country West is as much a style of today as it is a colorfully embroidered legacy of our past. It is cowboy charisma and down-home rusticity in a country homestead. It is native Indian crafts and desert colors in a city apartment. It is the use of building techniques and materials, whether in a new adobe or a restored mountain cabin, that are appropriate and authentic—*honest*—for dwelling and site alike.

American Country West is East meets West and West travels East. It is our English, European, Mexican, and Indian heritages coming together to create a look that is uniquely and genuinely American.

American Country West is a style that springs from the collective experience of the

WESTERN VALENTINE (*left*) was painted for all to see on the roof of a Colorado barn.

ENDURING FOLK HERO (*above*), the American cowboy, continues to lasso the West with the same skill and bravado celebrated in legends.

hundreds of thousands of men and women who left the relative security of the established eastern seaboard to settle the uncharted territories west of the Mississippi. It was through their encounters with the land, the forces of nature, and the native American civilizations that a western culture was first shaped; one that we celebrate here in this book.

These early settlers were an odd lot of marauders, adventurers, and family folk all in search of the same thing, a better life. The New World wasn't even old yet and they had already decided it was time to pack up and head west. Traveling overland by wagon train, they took few possessions with them. Their only valuables were the knowledge stored in their heads and the skills of their hands.

These settlers were unprepared for the extremes of the land and the weather. To come upon the Grand Canyon, the Mojave Desert, the Badlands, or the Rocky Mountains in the dead of winter or the blaze of summer was a cruel surprise. They met the challenges of their journey with courage, and when they had finally arrived at their destinations, they made homes, albeit primitive ones, to protect themselves and their families as best they could.

It is this struggle that is so dramatically imbued in the style of the West. It is seen in mesa Indian dwellings that capture the strength of the land and in early western houses—sod houses, adobes, log cabins, ranches, farms—which the settlers ingeniously wrought from the varied resources of arid deserts, rocky canyons, bald prairies, grassy plains, and verdant valleys.

The diverse geography of the West is celebrated in the names of its towns —Elephant Butte, New Mexico; Rimrock, Arizona; Levelland, Texas; Forestgrove, Montana; Boulder, Colorado—and in the artistry of Indian crafts whose geometric patterns seem to call up the lay of the land.

The wide-open spaces of the western range also spawned America's most enduring folk hero, the cowboy. And how this cowboy dressed, how he worked, how he amused himself, have provided many of the most unforgettable images of western culture.

The style called American Country West was born out of a newly discovered western pride. It is an explicit acknowledgment of the legacy of ancient Indian civilizations and their centuries-old skills. By resurrecting adobe building techniques, collecting early Indian artifacts, and

CHRIS MEAD

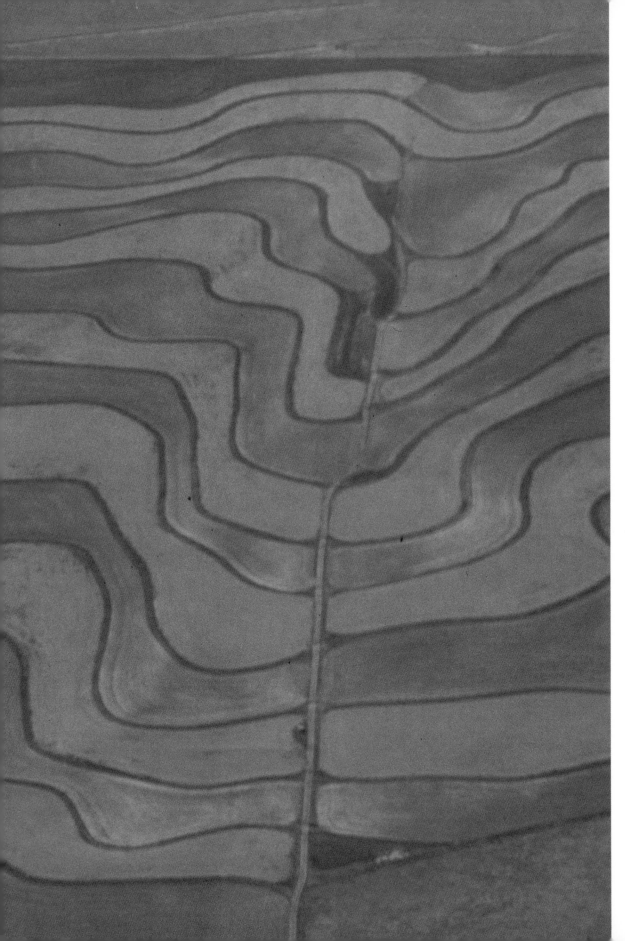

patronizing contemporary Indian artists and craftsmen, the style perpetuates the native American culture.

American Country West also celebrates the cowboy craftsmen whose output of utilitarian items—ropes, saddles, spurs, and belts—combine tradition, function, and art. It honors, too, the heritages that infuse the West—the inspired creations of such craftspeople as German cabinetmakers, Swedish log-cabin builders, Mexican tile artists, and Spanish ornamentalists.

More simply stated, American Country West is coming home to the needs of today out of a love and respect for the past.

PATTERNS OF THE WEST are found in an exquisite Navajo weaving (*far left*) and the aerial tapestry of a plowed western landscape (*left*).

9

DWELLINGS

EMERGE
FROM THE LAND

In the immense, sun-burnished land of the desert Southwest we find the origins of western style. For, ever since the Anasazi Indians (ancestors of modern Pueblo tribes) roamed the area some 2,000 years ago, the environment here has played a major role in shaping life, art, and architecture.

The earliest known dwellings—pit houses dug out of the ground—were adaptations of rudimentary food-storage cellars for newly cultivated maize. Soon after came crude aboveground mesa dwellings made of mud and small timber—the terraced building blocks of Pueblo civilization and a native architectural style of the same name.

MONUMENT VALLEY, ARIZONA (*left*), stark and unforgiving, supported human life 10,000 years ago.

MESA DWELLING (*right*) is among the Indian homes that still inhabit the terrain today.

Colors
OF THE WEST

The western landscape is a rich mosaic of color and texture that varies dramatically from region to region. Whether it is the result of nature rearranged for the convenience of man, as in a cactus fence planted to keep critters out, or of nature left to itself, as in a field of blazing purple wild flowers, the sight is impressive.

For centuries, Indians have drawn on the land for colors to enhance their art. Similarly, today's settlers look to the bleached hues of the desert, the deep seasonal colors of the mountains, and the intense blue of the omnipresent "big sky" to re-create the western landscape in their homes.

WESTERN HORTICULTURE, in its diversity of color and form, has been a source of inspiration for native artisans.

DICK ROWAN ▶

CHRIS MEAD ▶

NEWLY ROLLED HAY is a portrait of color and texture in a rural Texas field and also a practical way for the farmer to eliminate his need for a barn.

Animal Afterlife
IN THE WEST

Nothing is casually discarded in the West; everything has an afterlife. Skulls, antlers, and skins are familiar sights. Placed on a roof to bleach in the sun, or matter-of-factly nailed to a barn, they become graceful elements of the native decoration.

There's a playfulness to their use as well, as witness the antlers that transform a bare trunk into a handsome hat tree. Some pioneer families gathered the antlers shed by moose, elk, and deer not for a practical purpose but simply out of esteem for the natural processes of the wild. More utilitarian are the animal hides, sources of warmth in winter and a key material for the first upholsterers of the Old West.

SKULLS, ANTLERS, AND SKINS are an integral part of the western landscape. It is not uncommon to see animal afterlife curling around a tree, embellishing the side of a barn, or serving as an unexpected arbor or archway.

MAIN STREET WEST.
While the sun still sets
on pueblos as in ancient
times (*below*), a new
breed of motorized
Mustangs, Colts, and
Broncos line frontier
towns (*right*), hitch-
ing themselves to imagi-
nary posts.

FROM PUEBLO TO
SETTLEMENT

For Indian and pioneer alike, the message of the western frontier was the same: band together or perish. The land was too formidable to be controlled by man alone; many hands were needed to survive.

Precursors of modern apartment complexes, the community centers of the Pueblo Indians were compact clusters of adjoining rooms piled up to five-story heights. Constructed of rock, sand, timber, foliage, and water, the settlements, which came to be known as pueblos, were located atop mesas, in cliffside caverns, and on canyon floors.

Frontier towns provided pioneers with the sense of community that isolated farms and ranches could not. Plain wood buildings were gussied up with "false front" façades to evoke the grandeur—and stability—of remembered Main Streets back east.

Mountain Men

The mountain men of the 19th century stalked the wilderness with a predator's skill and an entrepreneur's ambition. They set out to make their fortunes by trapping for fur in the Rocky Mountains, choosing adventure rather than convention. They preferred to face down a grizzly bear over reporting to work every day in an "honest job."

In the Far West today, a new breed of mountain men is answering the call of the wild. Although these men do hold "honest jobs," on weekends they shed their professional roles, put on their fur pelt hats and Hudson Bay blanket coats, and set forth to relive the traditions of the original mountain men. They camp out in teepees, hunt and fish for food, and test their skills at surviving in the wilderness. By doing so, they honor the rugged individuals whose feats of stamina and bravado helped clear the way for the great westering movement.

20

MODERN MOUNTAIN MEN in the 20th-century West practice the same traditions as the original mountain men—weekends only.

WYOMING PEAKS are weekend homes to rugged mountain men.

THE SALOON
Western
TROPHY ROOM

For as long as cow-hands have been thirsty, there have been saloons on the muddy Main Streets of western towns. They provided a cama-raderie more sustaining than the effects of whis-key, fortifying early westerners against the challenges of their frontier.

Vividly furnished with images of the territory, the bars offer pictures of rodeoing and ranching, animals frozen in stances only a taxidermist on a hoot could create, assorted cowboy memo-rabilia, and the black-ened hieroglyphics of hot branding irons. These are the real trophy rooms of the West, behind whose swinging doors western swagger was refined to a perfect pitch.

NEON SIGNS aren't the only source of local color in western saloons. There are hunters' tro-phies, snakeskins, cow-boy memorabilia, and remnants of old advertis-ing campaigns to feast on while enjoying a beer.

25

GIMME CAP collection hangs from the ceiling of a Texas bar.

The early frontier churches were modest edifices, but there was nothing small about the role they played in the settling of the West. In a desolate new land fraught with danger, each church was a beacon of hope, a place of order and peace that provided pioneers with a chance to reaffirm an often sorely tested faith. The weekly Sunday meeting was also an occasion to gossip and to exchange information about the practical details of frontier life.

HOUSES OF WORSHIP reflect the same styles and influences as frontier residences. In Colorado, they may be dressed up with carpenter Victorian detail, in rural Texas, dressed down with a plain, no-nonsense façade. In the Southwest, churches and missions are cast in adobe; in Wyoming, it's not surprising to come upon a New England clapboard style.

29

Fencing
IN THE WEST

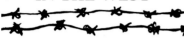

Zigzagging across the western landscape is the ever-present country fence. Whether built of tree limbs, split rail, weathered pickets, or barbed wire, the fence has served to keep animals in and trespassers, both the four-footed and two-footed varieties, out.

Pride of ownership is evident in the gateways of the West. With simple native materials, these portals make use of their spectacular settings and create a grand impression.

WESTERN BORDERS, whether ingeniously devised, like a twig fence woven with a basket-maker's finesse, or wittily conceived like a barrier made of live cactus, offer a panoply of imaginative styles and practical solutions for fencing in land.

30

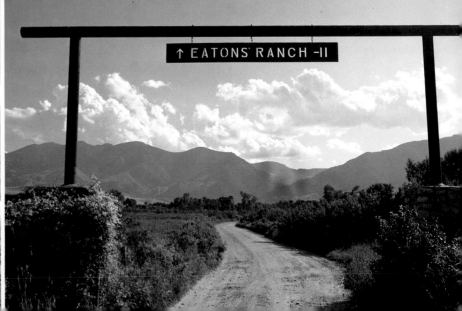

Homes
ON THE RANGE

In the western landscape, house styles read like road signs. It is evident when leaving the rural countryside of Texas for the arid desert of New Mexico, as native limestone, sloping roofs, and porches give way to native clay, flat adobe roofs, and *portales,* or covered porches.

Each style—adobe, log cabin, farmhouse, Spanish hacienda, and their variations—expresses a vernacular, which has taken form out of the local resources, concessions to the climate and terrain, and the influence of the native and immigrant cultures.

HOUSES OF THE WEST (*clockwise from top right*): a rustic Colorado log cabin, an ornate California Victorian residence, a German Texas cabin, a *fachwerk* gardener's shed, a 19th-century Texas farmhouse built of native wood, and a flat-roofed adobe.

DICK ROWAN ▶

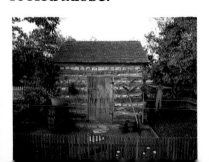

DOOR-TO-DOOR
WEST

The doors of the West convey many things: the colors in the local terrain, the effects of time and weather, and the influence of native cultures. Like a friendly handshake, these doors leave the impression that warmth and comfort lie within.

COLORFUL CALLING CARDS of the American West, doors can be crafted from native woods, left natural to blend with the scenery, painted to stand out against a monochromatic background, embellished with revival details like an Anglo-colonial pediment on a Spanish-colonial door, or decorated with characteristic native symbols or folk art.

35

2

Homes
of
the West

ADOBES

The prehistoric Indians were the first to mix native clay with water, and bonding materials like grasses and straw, to make adobe mud. Allowed to bake under the relentless western sun, the mud became the traditional building material of the Southwest.

STUDIO CONCEIVED AS ART (*left and preceding pages*), like John Nieto's large-scale work, is "a celebration of the beauty of Indian culture." Legendary Santa Fe light illuminates the room through an 8-foot window wall behind the artist. Next to the door made of local woods is an Indian "spirit hole."

Early earth-walled, conical structures were formed using adobe applied in successive layers. Later, the simple rectangular room plan evolved that laid the foundation for the pueblo style, our most familiar native American architecture. Spanish settlers are often credited with introducing a variation in technique. They poured mud into wooden molds to shape the traditional thick adobe brick.

Subsequently, as the influx of new peoples continued and control of the territories wavered under different flags, a multitude of regional styles emerged. But always at the core of these early styles, and their contemporary successors, is the same adobe technique that primitive Indians used to build their shelters thousands of years ago.

A STUDIO RICH IN ARTIST'S APACHE HERITAGE

This adobe was born of heaven and earth. Its spiritual origins are derived from artist John Nieto's Mescalero Apache forebears and its natural origins from the New Mexico earth.

Nieto sculpted, by hand and by hatchet, the malleable adobe brick into a dwelling that appears as though it has always been a part of the environment. "My ancestors have lived here for hundreds of years," he

PASSIVE SOLAR GLASS WALL (*below*) overlooks a terrace paved with local flagstone.

HAND-SCULPTED ADOBE DWELLING (*left*) was given its shape by Nieto, who carved his studio out of the soft brick. The natural terrace was formed with rock blasted from the site and relaid by hand.

39

says. "I just wanted something right for them and for the area, not something made of steel."

In his studio, Nieto surrounds himself with reminders of his heritage. The aperture cut into the wall next to the front door is a "spirit hole" found in ancient Indian dwellings, a passageway for good and evil spirits. His sleeping quarters above the fireplace are a facsimile of temporary lofts constructed over campfires by Indian shepherds in the wild.

In almost ceremonial chambers there appears to be no break between the prehistoric past and the present.

HORSESHOE-SHAPED WALL (*left*) divides the studio space and expresses an Indian belief that circular rather than angular openings welcome "god spirits." The deerskin resting on an Indian blanket is matter-of-fact native decoration.

SLEEPING LOFT (*right*) is made of Ponderosa pine with willow twig railing. It is an adaptation of an Indian shepherd's outdoor bedroom.

NATIVE AMERICANA IN SANTA FE

This playful New Mexican set-piece commemorates the Old West just as it celebrates the New West in a style that is both modern and faithful to regional traditions. It's the kind of style that permits a saddle to ride herd over a room filled with reminders of western culture: Mexican Colonial furniture, Indian pottery, Navajo blankets, and other native American objects.

"We looked four and a half years for this house," says Santa Fe gallery owner Elaine Horwitch

TOOLED SADDLE (*left*), inspired by the design of a Navajo "Eye Dazzler" blanket, creates an unexpected focal point in this Santa Fe living room. The saddle is a work of western art by Slim Green (see page 198).

who, after three decades living in the West, is still awed by her surroundings. "It's the space. The land we ride our horses on, the high desert, the mountains. The bigness is all around us."

The house is big, too, but what makes it unique is the superb craftsmanship of its construction. Indeed, the house is a work of art in itself, and so a most fitting backdrop for a formidable collection of contemporary south-

western and American art, the hallmark of Elaine Horwitch's galleries in Santa Fe and Scottsdale, Arizona.

The original frescoes painted on the dining-room walls by local Indian artists were an additional bonus that

43

came with the house. They offer an idealized portrait of early farm life in New Mexico and create a picturesque background for dining. The English buffet and Oriental rug are as at home here as the newly made Mexican dining table and chairs or the whimsical collection of Mojave ceramic dolls.

SOUTHWESTERN LIVING ROOM (*above*) combines Mexican Colonial furniture with native American objects and contemporary southwestern and American art.

44

INDIAN SCOOKURN DOLL (*right*) is named "Sam" and originally welcomed visitors to an Indian curio shop.

POTTERY AND BASKET COLLECTION (*below*), which decorates an early New Mexican table, like Topsy, just grew. Of special interest are the large Peruvian Schipvo pots and Apache "circus" basket, so-named for its elephant designs.

NAÏVE FRESCOES (*left*), painted by local Indians, offer a portrait of early New Mexican farm life. The house, built in 1928, is largely unchanged and remains a treasure of southwestern craftsmanship, as the dining room bears out.

PRE-1900 MOJAVE CERAMICS (*right*), and a smattering of pre-Columbian objects, embellish the dining room hearth.

PINE TABLE is the hub of the enlarged kitchen that also features a 10-foot-long buffet, built-in sofa, and cozy hearth.

The kitchen is the only part of the house that had to be remodeled to accommodate the large-scale entertaining enjoyed by the owners. The new kitchen is 40 feet long and sports a coved ceiling with skylights. Double doors open onto the patio where summer parties are a tradition and views of the mountain landscape are savored between courses.

WELL-USED MEXICAN TABLE (*left*), circa 1900, along with a Kilim runner and copper pots, lend rustic charm to a kitchen with all the modern conveniences.

BEADED NOVELTIES (*above*) represent a collection that spans the early 1900s to the 1940s and includes bags, gloves, ties, and collars. They are mostly the work of northwestern coastal Indians. "When I started collecting these," says the owner, "nobody paid much attention to them." Today, many are considered museum-quality.

WOODEN BEAMS that traverse the garden-room fireplace (*above*) are brightened with decorative painting by local Indians. Flat Kachina-like figures are primitive Woletto Indian art.

CHEST PAINTED WITH WESTERN SCENES (*left*) is northern New Mexican Indian folk art from the 1920s.

51

LIFE-SIZED FOLK-ART GIRAFFES (*left*) are unexpected visitors to the patio area. The portal is made from native woods and twig-style chairs are the creation of a local Santa Fe artisan known only as "Pancho."

The patio is enlivened by native folk art at its most whimsical—life-size carved wood giraffes and cigar-store Indians. "I collect a lot of things because I think they're funny or clever," says the owner. "You can't be deadly serious about everything!"

CIGAR STORE INDIAN AND UNCLE SAM (*above*) stand in front of the house. Wooden Indians were commonplace sights in the West, but Uncle Sam is a more unusual figure.

53

TRADITIONAL CRAFTSMANSHIP
IN A REMODELED ADOBE

As an artist, Rosalea Murphy lives for the light. And her Santa Fe studio with its 20-foot-tall ceilings and high northern windows, the light never fails to inspire.

The ceiling is a hallmark of southwestern craftsmanship. The use of *vigas*, massive hori-

CARVED HORSE (*left*) from old Mexico perches with the same grace as a balcony atop a massive beam.

PINK ADOBE PROPRIETOR Rosalea Murphy (*below*), an artist as well as a restaurateur, owns the popular Santa Fe gathering spot for sampling regional specialties.

ANCIENT INDIAN ROCK PAINTING was the inspiration for Agnes Sims's petroglyph (*above*), hanging over the living-room sofa. Colorful Navajo blankets are casually draped on the furniture.

zontal timber beams placed on top of thick adobe walls, and *latillas,* smaller strips or planks of wood laid between the beams, oftentimes in a herringbone design, is a construction technique perfected by the early Indians to support heavy earthen roofs.

When Murphy moved to Santa Fe from Dallas, Texas, in 1940, the town reminded her of a small Mexican village: "There weren't any paved streets," she recalls, "and people bought firewood off the backs of burros." Her house, built some-time shortly after World War I, retains its original quaintness, though, like Santa Fe, it, too, has grown over the years. The studio was added, living room enlarged, and kitchen remodeled.

"I love to cook as much as I love to paint," says Murphy about a kitchen that was made to order for showcasing her culinary talents and the talents of another artist in the family—Murphy's daughter Priscilla Hoback (see page 213), whose stoneware is proudly displayed on the open kitchen shelving.

HANDMADE PINE CAB-
INETS, Mexican tile
backsplash, antique
Welsh dresser, and con-
temporary southwestern
stoneware plates, bowls,
and cups (*above*) lend the
kitchen a rough-cast
quality.

TWIG BORDER (*right
and far right*), which once
kept coyotes out, fences
in seasonal color. Like
everything else in Santa

Fe, gardening is infor-
mal, with the emphasis
on wild flowers and pot-
ted blooms that enjoy
lots of sun.

57

A RESTORED ADOBE HACIENDA WITH AN
Ancient Past

Time stands still at Casa San Ysidro, a rare 18th-century Spanish adobe hacienda in Corrales, New Mexico, restored and reconstructed by historian Alan Minge and his wife, Shirley. Once, however, time threatened to completely obliterate Casa Ysidro. "The house was in pretty bad condition when we bought it in 1952," reports Dr. Minge, "with only about a third of the building remaining." To the Minges' surprise, a foundation of much greater proportions than the visible structure was discovered in the ruins. Further

WHITEWASHED PINE CEILINGS and earth-colored walls (*left*) are among many period details of the 18th-century Spanish New Mexican hacienda reconstructed from a buried foundation. It is authentically furnished with regional antiques.

BLUE CAST-IRON STOVE (*left*), **from the 1800s, now stands in the reconstructed kitchen. The appliance was originally shipped from Colorado to Santa Fe and transported by wagon train to a family of weavers in Chimayo, New Mexico.**

ADZ-CARVED CORBEL (*left*) **caps a cottonwood column supporting a** *portal*, **a traditional Spanish porch.**

ADOBE CORRAL (*left*), **a common building type for housing domestic animals on a hacienda of this size, was moved to the property by the owners.**

59

excavations uncovered pottery shards that indicated the site had been occupied by Indians as early as the 13th century.

It was with more than a passing interest in the past that the Minges began the reconstruction of their hacienda. As a scholar specializing in the study of Hispanic and southwestern native American cultures, Dr. Minge had a professional curiosity about the place. The Minges rebuilt the hacienda to its original size and specifications using the newly discovered foundation as their blueprint. Minge did much of the work himself, reviving traditional adobe construction methods. "I learned a lot from my Hispanic neighbors," he notes. "The old-timers especially have been a lot of help—and my biggest supporters." Minge feels particularly indebted for a technique to color walls that relies on using different earth deposits around New Mexico.

SHIPPING CHEST (*below*), which carried freight between Santa Fe and Mexico in the 1600s, sits in the gallery. The painted pine chair is 19th-century New Mexican. Made for the Minges by a friend, the rag rug is in the style of a *jerga*, a traditional floor covering from the 18th and 19th centuries.

COPPER CASSO (*right*), dated 1689, is part of a rare collection of antique household items. The pot sits in the center of the hearth where early Spaniards cooked the family meals. The bold patterned rug, colored by vegetable dyes, is Navajo.

The owners' insistence on authenticity led them to reclaim period woodwork and artifacts from many abandoned adobes in the area. "I was amazed to discover how little interest there was at the time in collecting household items and furniture from the 1700s," notes Dr. Minge. The Minge collection of regional antiques documents an era of New Mexican life that otherwise might have been lost.

SINGLE-STORY HACIENDA (*left*) was introduced by Spanish colonialists in New Mexico. In many ways it is reminiscent of the pueblo building style; both are made of adobe and laid out by eye.

PRIMITIVE BENCH (*top*), made in New Mexico, is circa 1800 and still has its original coat of paint.

EARLY HARINERO (*above*) under the kitchen portal is a grain storage chest unique to New Mexico.

63

NEW MEXICAN SKY surrounds "House of Clouds,"
a newly constructed adobe in the old tradition.

ADOBE
IN THE CLOUDS

Just as artist Eric Sloane's landscape paintings and his writings—such keenly focused books as *For Spacious Skies, Seasons of America Past, Legacy,* and *Age of Barns*—pay homage to the American countryside, so does *Casa de las Nubes,* House of Clouds, pay homage to a native American style.

Great care was taken by the Sloanes during construction of the house to ensure adobe authenticity. "The walls are three and one half feet thick, all the way around," stressed Sloane, who died in March 1985. Although the exterior mood is strictly southwestern as a result, much of the expression inside comes from old

OUTSIZED SKULL (*above*) is an imposing presence at the entrance to artist Eric Sloane's studio. The Indian word *kiva*, inscribed on the door, refers to the sacred Pueblo ceremonial chambers on which Sloane modeled his atelier.

65

WATER TROUGH, old yoke, and checkerboard (*above*), **are practical objects arranged as for a still life.**

DISCARDED STIRRUP is an amusing pull for the rustic door (*right*) **that provides a New England welcome in New Mexico.**

66

New England—a reflection of Eric Sloane's steadfast loyalty to his Connecticut Yankee roots. (The Sloanes maintained another home in Cornwall, Connecticut.) "Everything adapts very well here

CARVED CORBELS, round *vigas*, and herringbone *latillas* (*above*), braces, beams, and wood strips are authentic southwestern ceiling details. The corbels, made from native ponderosa pine, have a twofold function: to decorate and to support the weight of the heavy beams.

IRON PIECES (*left*) and assorted gizmos from New England add a Yankee brand of early Americana to an adobe wall.

and soon begins to look native," he notes.

As a young man, when Eric Sloane first visited the Southwest, it was the sky that impressed him the most. And the sky soon became the important theme in his life's work. Numerous paintings depict New Mexican and New England "cloudscapes"; a word he coined to describe his fascination.

From a site that affords a view of not one but four mountain ranges, the sky never escapes notice. "You don't have to look up to see the clouds," says Mimi Sloane, "you are surrounded by them."

A SPANISH HACIENDA WITH AN
Indian Character

The late Millicent Rogers discovered Taos, New Mexico, in the 1940s when it was still a mecca for artists, craftsmen, and their benefactors. D. H. Lawrence, Mabel Dodge, Dorothy Brett, and others had come there beginning in the 1920s to live and work in rustic seclusion.

Mrs. Rogers, the Standard Oil heiress and life-long art patron, was so enchanted by the Pueblo culture of the remote village that she commissioned local Indian artisans to build her residence in their native style. However, when a buried foundation was unearthed at the start of construction, indicating a four-walled building of early Spanish origin, Mrs. Rogers had the Indians rebuild the house following the foundation lines.

GRINDING STONES (*above*), **used originally to produce flour, now serve as poolside sculptures.**

RECONSTRUCTED HACIENDA (*far left*), **like Pueblo missions, reflects a combination of Spanish and Indian building styles. The blunted edges, rounded corners, and** *vigas* **protruding through the adobe walls are characteristic Indian details; the archways and four-walled plan, Spanish.**

CHEVRON-PATTERN PLANK DOOR (*left*) **was retrieved from an abandoned 200-year-old adobe building.**

69

"The house is actually two cultures—Indian and Spanish—expressed as one architecture," explains Mrs. Rogers's son, Arturo Peralta-Ramos, who with his wife, Jackie, resides here. Originally, it was thought that the building, with its ammunition room and six-foot-thick firewall, had been a 16th-century fortress. More recent evidence suggests that it was a hacienda of 18th-century vintage.

TAOS ANIMAL FRES-COES (*below and left*), **painted by Indian artist Joseph Swazo, are ephemeral portraits of wildlife once common to the southwestern land-scape.**

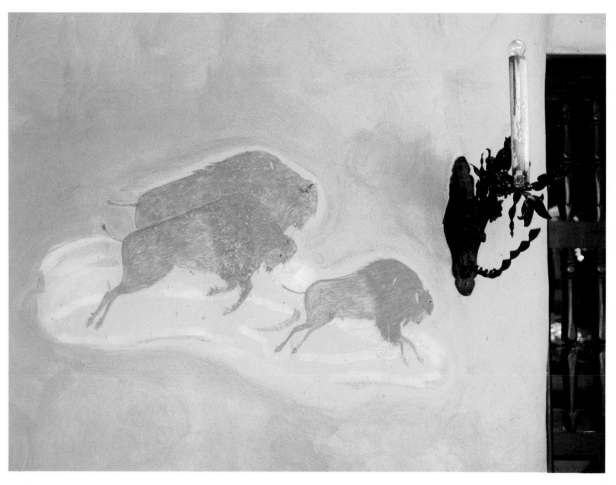

FORMAL PORTAL (*left*), **surrounding a courtyard lush with New Mexican flora, has columns with Indian designs painted on them by Millicent Rogers. Corbels, used as decorative braces, have been embellished with drawings of fanciful animals left behind by house guests such as Clark Gable, Gary Cooper, and Ian Fleming.**

71

The Ramos family's interest in preserving the Taos culture is apparent in their collection of indigenous American art and objects, which fills the house, mixing comfortably with furniture and art from many other cultures.

"The soft, white adobe walls are kind to everything you put in the room," observes Jackie Ramos. "A more decorative setting would be inappropriate for the primitive Indian pieces."

PLASTERED ADOBE WALLS enhance a display of native American artifacts (*left*) that includes baskets, Kachina dolls, and weavings made by Northwest, Central Plains, and Southwest Indians.

INDIAN-STYLE BEE-HIVE HEARTHS (*far left, left, and below*) **keep rooms warm all through the night due to the heat retention properties of the adobe brick.**

LEGENDARY BAD GUY of the Wild West is chronicled in hooked rug (*below*). **This style of storytelling was transported from New England, where it had long been a traditional folk art.**

A KINDLY MAN WAS JESSIE JAMES
AND THOUGHTFUL OF THE POOR
HED STEAL A SHIRT FROM OFF YOUR BACK
TO HELP A MAN NEXT DOOR
I DONT BELIVE IN SINFUL WAYS
OR TO DIE UNTIL ONES SHRIVEN
BUT A MAN LIKE MR JAMES DESERVES
SOME LITTLE SEOT IN HEAVEN

EARTH-HUGGING CACTUS GARDEN (*above and left*) is as southwestern as it is Far Eastern in appearance. Slabs of native rock provide the perch from which to contemplate a prickly Oriental garden. Cushions, the thickness of adobe walls, turn a ledge into an inviting banquette.

Traditional
ADOBE WITH ORIENTAL DETAILS

Alexander and Susan Girard modestly call this "an adobe with no particular style." In fact, it is a contemporary house distinguished as much by its scrupulous sense of design as by its imposing serenity.

The building is a southwestern adobe suffused, surprisingly, with an Oriental mood.

GALLERY OF MANY CULTURES (*above*) includes a multinational mix of art and artifacts. In the hall is a life-sized sculpture by Mexican artist Teodora Blanco, a French café table, an American solid log chair with an unexpected valentine, and doors solidly overlaid with brass disks from India.

WOODEN CROSS INLAID WITH BONE, a remarkable piece of folk art crafted by the owner, occupies a special niche in the object wall created to house a spectrum of folk pieces. An African bed serves as a bench; the stool next to it is also African.

The cactus plantings bring to mind a rock garden bonsai. The gallery hall, with its gilded door and sculpted Indian figure suggests the entrance of a Taoist shrine.

After years of living in New York and abroad, the Girards made Santa Fe their home, and the city's Museum of International Folk Art home to their magnificent collection of some 100,000 miniatures from more than a hundred countries. Like the museum collection, their residence reflects a fastidious and unerring appreciation for detail. It is a visual narrative of objects and art set off by pure light and space, but mostly it is an environment that represents the culling of a lifetime's avocation down to the most essential basics.

PUEBLO CHURCH FOLK MINIATURE (*below*), 18 inches tall, was made by the owner out of wood and decorated with silver ex votos, symbol offerings to the supernatural.

CAST-IRON ORNAMENTAL HOUSE (*below*) is a 19th-century coin bank from a collection of architectural objects. In the living room, which is washed in white backgrounds and New Mexican light, art provides the color.

DESERT
STONEHENGE

"Must sell my beautiful pile of boulders near Carefree, AZ" read the ad. A visit by Bill and Sunnie Empie to the site resulted in an immediate decision to buy this desert Stonehenge where, a few years later, they built one of the most unusual residences anywhere. New Mexican architect Charles Foreman Johnson, commissioned by the Empies to design a house around the granite boulders, must have felt at times that he was reinventing a shelter first envisioned centuries ago by ancient Indians.

Johnson's pueblo-style plan incorporates passageways and rooms as dictated by the position of the rocks, and maximizes use of the site's layout and materials. Custom-fitted glass seals the natural openings, but dawn's early light still pours through them

GIGANTIC GRANITE BOULDERS (*left and right*) defined the form of the adobe set into the desert landscape.

as it did hundreds of thousands of years ago.

When traditional adobe was ruled out as a building material (it could not bond with steel-reinforced granite), concrete blocks were painstakingly made to look like adobe, plastered with layers of stucco that were hand-troweled and sand-finished.

DRIED CACTUS RIBS laced with rawhide (*below left*) are ingenious natural window blinds.

COPPER AND GLASS DOOR (*below*) by Federico Armijo evokes the entrance to an ancient Hohokam cave discovered on the site.

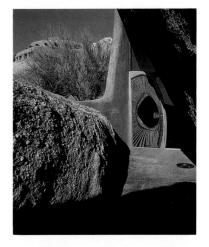

Even the colors in the house's interior and exterior paints were matched to samples of stone and earth gathered from the site. "The house itself rejected anything that wasn't natural or native," says Mrs. Empie, who conceived the interior design plan.

ORGANIC MATERIALS and sculpted shapes (*left*) give native definition to the 20th-century cave dwelling.

SHAFT OF GLASS seals a natural crack between the boulders (*right*). The red fir ladder wrapped in rawhide adds a Pueblo Indian detail. The primitive jar is Papago pottery; the rug, Navajo.

TALL NATIVE CACTUS (*below right*) stands near wall of weathered granite. On the floor are Hohokam and Papago storage *ollas*, and, standing against the wall, an early Mexican chest.

PRIMITIVE MEXICAN TABLE (*below far right*) displays southwestern pottery, a ceramic sculpture by Glen La Fontaine, and branding-iron candlesticks.

HAND-SHAPED FIRE-PLACE (*left*) embellishes the dining room, where the antique table and leather-covered chairs come from Spain.

MEXICAN TRASTERO (*above*), from the late 19th century, fits in a natural niche.

HAND-SCULPTED CONCRETE (*above right*) was plastered to resemble adobe and colored to match the earth.

WALNUT KITCHEN STOOLS (*right*) by artist Dale Broholm seem as naturally formed as the boulders. Oak cabinets were sandblasted to emphasize the wood's horizontal grain.

Log Houses

LOG HOUSES

Crude one-room log cabins constructed of pine, spruce, oak, fir, redwood, or whatever local timber was available were the first permanent shelters on the frontier. The early settlers felled the trees by ax then built cabins on a four-corner plan, relying on the tried-and-true techniques first brought to colonial America by Swedish immigrants in the 17th century. Logs were laid horizontally and joined at the corners by a variety of notching techniques ranging from the simple saddle notch to the more complicated full dovetail.

By the late 1800s, railroads had opened up the West, and, with the availability of all types of building materials, the log cabin was freed from its heavy proportions and boxy shape. Bulky frames were replaced by two-by-four balloon frames, hand-hewn logs by milled sheathing, and notched joints by metal nails.

Whether newly built or restored, precisely engineered or intentionally rough-cast, prefabricated or artistically handcrafted, the log house today continues to endure. Combining simplicity and ingenuity, these buildings are powerful reminders of the pioneer culture.

TEXAS GERMAN LOG CABIN (*left*) from 1856 was modernized, but, through the use of old materials, retains its period charm.

GERMAN LOG CABIN IN THE Heart of Texas HILL COUNTRY

Except for the occasional television antenna sticking up, Fredericksburg, Texas, in the rolling farmlands between Austin and San Antonio, remains the picture of a 19th-century German country village. Founded in 1846 by a group of settlers sponsored by the

LOG CABIN PRIVY (*below*) is a newly built bathroom for the use of guests.

SUN-BLEACHED SKULLS (*below*) from the countryside mingle easily with potted cactus plants on the porch.

FACHWERK WALL
(*above*), set off by a
native stone fireplace, is
made of local oak and
plastered limestone.

TEXAS HORN CHAIR AND TABLE (*below*), with matching child's chair, are reproductions of an early furniture style popular in cattle-ranching areas. Deerskin rugs and hunting trophies reflect the sporting traditions of the region, and the cedar chest, the woodworking traditions of German immigrants. The locally made ladder leads to a sleeping loft.

Society for the Protection of German Immigrants, and today used as a country retreat by many Texas city folk, the town has never lost touch with its German heritage. "You don't find just a trace of tradition here, it pervades everything," says the owner of the 1856 log cabin, which has been carefully enlarged to meet 20th-century needs.

CYPRESS LADDER AND BED (*left*) **are examples of Fredericksburg craftsmanship. On the bed is an antique coverlet from Kentucky.**

Like the Texan spoken here, local crafts, cuisine, and architecture are heavily accented by German. This cabin's *fachwerk* style is a variation on a remembered homeland design, adapted to materials abundant in this area such as oak and limestone. "We're very distant from our regular city lives here," says the cabin owner by way of explaining the time-capsule effect of residing in Fredericksburg. "We can take the time to do things the long way," from making local specialties like sausage to washing dishes. "We had a dishwasher installed when we moved in, but we've never used it."

ROLLING PIN BED (*below*) **is German and named for the rounded design of the headboard and footboard. The cabinet, also German, originally came with screen panels, which were replaced by fabric.**

TIMBERED
Tour de Force
IN THE
ROCKY MOUNTAINS

High in the Colorado Rockies sits a family compound crafted with an artistry as enthralling as the scenery encircling it. Steve Cappellucci, a gifted woodworker, transformed an ordinary 1950s summer cabin into an extraordinary homestead, then hand-built a guest house, barn, and workshop to go with it.

The new structures were made of native timber with pegged-beam ceilings. The guest house has dovetailed log walls. Hand-split poles were used for the trim on doors and windows and twigs were ingeniously fashioned into cabinet handles.

Before being upholstered with fabric, the interior walls of the main

HANDCRAFTED CABIN (*far left*) is a man-made embellishment of the natural wonders of the mountain site. HOLLOWED-OUT LOGS (*above*) serve as window boxes. OLD COPPER COOKING POT (*left*) simmers with Rocky Mountain color.

93

house first had to be sheetrocked. One of the owners recalls coming upon a worker's notation on an unfinished section: "February 23, a perfectly beautiful day."

"A house that has received this much love and attention," she remarks, "can't help but be a happy place." For the family, part of the joy in spending summers in the mountains is sharing the experience with

JUTTING REDWOOD DECK (*above*) brings the beauty of nature within reach. The hearth is surrounded by benches, tables, and railings handcrafted of lodgepole pine.

friends. "We like to get up by the middle of June in time to see the calves and ducklings and young beavers and to enjoy the fishing. My husband will rise at four in the morning to catch a dinner for twenty."

GNARLED WOOD (*above*) has been incorporated as a natural architectural brace. Pegs are improvised from tree branches.

HAND-HEWN PINE POSTS AND BARS (*above*) provide a sturdy yet elegant porch railing.

HOLLOWED STUMP, TROUGH, AND BARREL (*above left, left, and above*) display the gardening know-how of the builder's wife, Chris.

TREE-STUMP STOOL (*above*) was made by Cappellucci's grandfather and teacher, David Work.

95

MARBLE "COLD CLOSET" (*above*), or pantry, is also a workspace for drying flowers and herbs.

PINE CABINETS (*left*) conceal a modern kitchen's functions; even the refrigerator (*below*) is artfully disguised.

TWO-SIDED HEARTH (*left and below*), made of local stone, separates formal and informal areas of the living room. Handcrafted bookcases exhibit unusual attention to detail.

SPECKLED TIMBER (*right*), the result of randomly peeling bark, is used for the bedroom ceiling beams, window trim, and headboard.

HAND-HEWN ARCH (*right*) consists of four pieces of spruce bound together by wood pegs and wrought-iron tie rods custom-made by local ironmaker Nick Brumder.

The guest house was Steve Cappellucci's most ambitious undertaking. "He had dreamed of building a house with handmade arches," says one of the owners, "so we just gave him carte blanche." The ceiling arches provide the main room of the house with a cathedral-like feeling and show Cappellucci's knack for precision joinery.

For the sides of the house, logs were first cut from standing dead spruce timber, then custom-milled into boards square on three sides, with one surface left curved and natural. The speckled finish on this surface was achieved through the strokes of Cappellucci's drawknife.

ENGLISH STAGHORN CHANDELIER (*right*), antique painted cupboard from Denmark, and wall-hung oxen yoke from France enhance the rustic mood of the guest house. Cooking island is fitted with handmade cabinets.

CURVED WINDOW LINTELS (*below*) in the dining room were fashioned from spruce logs. Retractable shades on the glass roof regulate the sunlight.

ANTIQUE WICKER LOVE SEAT AND CHAIRS (*left*) have old-fashioned floral cushions. A crude trough makes an offbeat serving table.

99

TWIG HEADBOARD (*above*) in the guest house was built by Cappellucci and inspired by a country fence.

"When you take most people for a drive in the country, they notice the mountains, the birds, or the flowers," explains one of the owners, "but Steve will notice how a particular tree grows and bends—and he'll remember it," returning to pluck from nature the arm of a chair, the back of a bench, or the base of a lamp.

FEED TROUGH (*left*), into which Mary Emmerling pitches hay, is another example of Cappellucci's sophisticated carpentry.

WORKING TACK (*below*) claims an appropriate roost in the barn.

SPRUCE LOG BARN and its six-rail paddock fence (*right*) received as much attention from the builder as did the main houses.

101

OLD OXEN YOKE (*above*), hanging from weathered logs that rest on columns of local stone, marks the spectacular entrance to MacDonald Becket's house in Sun Valley, Idaho.

AN IDAHO LOG HOUSE
MADE IN MONTANA

Everything about Aspen Meadows, the Sun Valley, Idaho, vacation residence of architect and builder MacDonald Becket, was influenced by a desire "to make this place as natural and beautiful as possible." Strip-mining holes on the property were converted into ponds stocked with fish. Some 300 young trees were planted and scrubland was replaced with four horse pastures.

The house itself was constructed from a custom kit. Lodgepole pine logs were cut, notched, and fitted in a Montana lumberyard, shipped to the site, then carefully reassembled. Becket stipulated a design using logs of uneven length in order to obtain the natural appearance he desired in the house. "To have

CATTLE SKULL (*right*) keeps company with a holiday wreath. LODGEPOLE PINE LOGS (*below*) were cut to different lengths and arranged in staggered rows.

CUSTOM KIT HOUSE (*right*) was modified by the owner to fit in with the surroundings and make the most of the views.

something more symmetrical in a log cabin would seem inappropriate," he explains.

The naturalistic style carries through to the interior space, where logs jut forth irregularly,

STONE-AND-TIMBER FIREPLACE (*left*), hand-built by an Indian stonemason from local materials, displays a huge buffalo trophy and delicate Indian quiver.

SIOUX TURKEY-FEATHER HEADDRESS and Nez Percé "wearing dress" (*below and right*), from the 1950s and 1920s respectively, clothe the house in authentic Indian garb.

and chinking applied between the logs is intentionally uneven. The Indian blankets, rugs, and ceremonial garments lend color and an informal tone consistent with relaxed mountain manners. "When I come up here, I get on what I call 'mountain time,' " explains Becket. "That means saying you'll be somewhere at nine but not showing up until ten—and nobody minds at all."

CHINKED LOG WALLS (*above right and above far right*) **are the backdrop for a pair of Navajo weavings. The saddle blanket dates from the 1920s and the red "Semi Dazzler" is from the 1880s.**

WELSH COUNTRY TABLE (*right*) **is a 19th-century pine piece; ladder-back chairs are English country reproductions, and the pine sideboard is American-made from the early 1900s.**

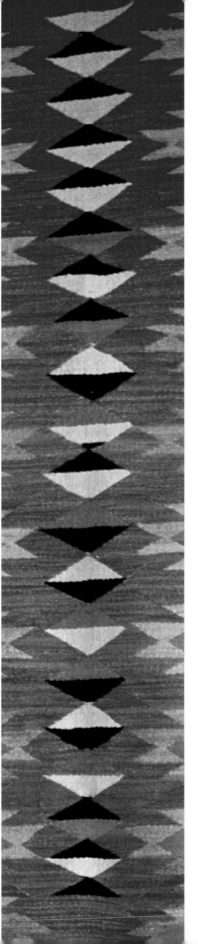

PINE-WALLED WESTERN SPA (*far left*) **has lap pool, Jacuzzi, and breathtaking views of mountains and sky.**

NAVAJO "SEMI DAZ-ZLER" (*above and left*), **circa 1900, accents the bedroom. Symbolic designs, such as the zig-zag pattern, are storytell-ing devices used by weavers to describe their history and their land.**

107

CASA
IN THE SUN VALLEY
MOUNTAINS

When Robert and Jackie Caywood moved to Sun Valley, Idaho, from Taos, New Mexico, they brought their New Mexican culture with them, and it has taken root and flourished in the mountains. The stuccoed exterior of the house calls to mind the adobes of Taos, which

SOD-ROOF LOG HOUSE in Sun Valley (*right*) was built with native timber, but its exterior was stuccoed to resemble adobe.

OAK BENCH topped with mirror (*below*) holds familiar signs of ranch life.

are also brought to mind by the terra-cotta tile floors, Indian-style fireplaces, and an extensive collection of American Indian artifacts.

Bob Caywood, his son, and friend, a retired carpenter, built the house entirely by hand. They went into the mountains to log their own fir and spruce timber, bringing it down five to six logs at a time to cut into the exact lengths they needed. The Forest Service sold them stands of dead timber. Twenty-four of these trees support the massive, hand-cut beams and a sod roof grown over with native vegetation. They even hauled rock from a local mountain rockslide to form the fireplace wall.

BEADWORK AND BASKETS (*left*) in a cabinet collection include Sioux, Cheyenne, Nez Percé, and Kiowa beaded items and turn-of-the-century Indian basketry. The Navajo saddle blanket on the table is circa 1870–1880.

LODGEPOLE PINE FURNITURE (*below*) is of local origin. Ledges, cleverly built into the fireplace wall, display historic Acoma and contemporary Zuñi pottery, along with a Hopi Kachina doll. The Navajo blanket was woven in the 1880s; the fringed burden basket is Apache.

ANTIQUE SPURS AND RAM'S SKULL (*above*) are western embellishments for a kitchen hearth inlaid with Mexican tiles. In the breakfast nook, a discarded wagon wheel has taken a new turn as a lighting fixture and hanging rack for plants.

HOPI AND TLINGIT BASKETS (*right*), from 1880 to 1900, predominate in this bookcase collection. The two Tlingit baskets (*fifth and sixth from the left*) are circa 1890 and show motifs of salmon laying eggs and a totemic design considered to be very rare.

110

The Caywood basket collection started by a fluke. A sixty-eight-year-old Indian woman who sold Bob some beadwork off the back of a truck casually mentioned that she had been collecting baskets ever since she was a girl. Eventually, Bob bought 112 baskets from her. Many of them are museum quality, but for now they are right at home in the house that the Caywoods built.

CARVED MEXICAN CHEST (*left*), set off by a Navajo "Eye Dazzler," circa 1870, holds a pair of Sioux moccasins from the late 1800s, a Seri Indian basket from Mexico, and a wood carving by New Mexican artist Leo Salazar. The pot sitting on the chest took first prize at the 1975 Indian Market in Santa Fe.

PEGGED FOUR-POSTER BED (*below*) is handmade from peeled lodgepole pine logs. The vegetal-dyed floor rug is a new Navajo; the other Navajos date from 1920.

LOCAL ROCK HEARTH (*below*) can be seen from the study where North American Indian objects—a Northwest Coast mask, Canadian beaded pipe, Hopi Kachina doll, antique baskets, and modern Pueblo pottery—decorate tabletops, shelves, and the Indian-style hearth.

UTAH MINER'S CABIN

Frank Magleby knew the unassuming cabin was right when he saw it —just as he recognizes a good subject when he comes upon it. A landscape painter and art professor, Magleby discovered this old miner's cabin standing on some property he had acquired in Sundance, Utah.

"My first idea was to rip the house apart, then rebuild it using the original foundation," he says. During the reconstruction, however, he decided to take a few liberties with the limited floor plan. He created a larger dwelling but remained faithful to the old cabin by incorporating weathered pine planking and rough-sawed lumber into the new design. The result is a home with a random, informal pattern not unlike the unscheduled existence his family likes to lead here.

KENTUCKY WILLOW CHAIRS (*above*) warm to a Utah fire. An old bobcat coat and Indian blanket are western lap throws. The rug on the floor is a new Indian weaving.

PINE SPINDLE BED, covered with an Amish quilt (*right*), is a Mormon piece of local origin; pine was the only wood available before the railroad came to Utah. The blanket chest is also pine but from Pennsylvania.

REBUILT MINER'S CABIN (*above*) was constructed from salvaged pine. Old farm tools from New England decorate the side of the house.

112

GOTHIC WINDOW NICHE (*below*) offers wilderness views from its built-in bench.

WESTERN PELTS AND YANKEE FARM TOOLS (*left*) share a wall; the biggest pelt is buffalo, the shaggy brown one is Icelandic sheepskin, and the goatskin comes from Spain. A lambskin throw drapes the sofa.

RUSTIC

MOUNTAIN CABIN FROM A KIT

Snug in the mountains of Sundance, Utah, this lodgepole pine log cabin, built from a kit, provides a family with a retreat from their hectic urban existence in Los Angeles. "This is where we come to relax, " says one of the owners. "I love hearing the trees rustle in the Chinook winds and seeing the deer come up to our windows."

Her husband, a noted director, discovered the area while on location for a film. Subsequently, the couple decided to make Sundance their home away from home.

TIMBERLINE CABIN (*above right, right, and far right*) in Sundance is a product of a kit by Alpine Log Homes. The lodgepole pine comes from an inventory of dry standing timber and is then hand-peeled and hand-notched into the components of a custom house.

COVERED ENTRY (*left*) was hand hewn using the owner's design and timber found on the property.

RAWHIDE-WRAPPED CROSSBEAMS (*left*) are a re-creation of a frontier technique used for securing logs.

115

SNOWSHOES, FUR PELTS, AND MOOSE ANTLERS (*left*) provide the main room of this mountain retreat with potent reminders of the surrounding wilderness.

OLD WAGON WHEEL (*right*) serves as a modern lighting fixture in the dining room.

INDIAN BASKETS (*below*) occupy a niche specially built for the display of native crafts.

BOW-AND-ARROW tote, brass bed, and roll-top desk (*right*) confer an Old West image on a new western bedroom.

Ranch
Houses

Ranch Houses

In 1843, a Scottish nobleman, Sir William Drummond, organized an excursion out of Kansas City for a group of wealthy easterners to hunt for buffalo and fish the lakes and streams of the West. The trip, a huge success with city slickers, launched a uniquely American tradition—the dude ranch vacation.

By the turn of the century, tenderfoot cowboys were signing up as paying guests at numerous western ranches, which were, simply, working ranches with appropriately comfortable bunk-

HIGH PEAKS AND MOUNTAIN MEADOWS (*preceding pages*) surround the Seven D Ranch, which is nestled in an isolated corner of the Sunlight Basin.

TIMBERWOLF PELTS, COWHIDE SKINS, AND NAVAJO RUGS (*left*) instill the spirit of the genuine West in the ranch's main lodge.

houses for guests. The city wranglers took great delight in mending fences, branding cattle, shoeing horses, sleeping in cabins, eating chuckwagon grub, and riding with real cowboys for a few weeks or months during the summer.

Today, dude ranches, now more often called guest ranches, continue to keep the wild, woolly West alive for new generations of visitors.

The working ranch, which has spawned so many western customs, also led indirectly to the development of an informal and genuinely American house style which came to be known as "ranch." Early versions

varied from region to region and relied heavily on local materials and labor. By the 1930s, a more standardized ranch style began to appear. The ubiquitous "ranch rambler" became the dominant residential building style throughout the country during the 1950s and 1960s.

Wyoming
HIGH COUNTRY
Ranch

Time has done little to alter the look of the Seven D Ranch in the remote Sunlight Basin near Cody, Wyoming.

The main lodge appears as it did in the 1920s when an illustrious clientele including Alice Longworth Roosevelt and the Marshall Field family of Chicago stepped off Pullman cars to spend summers there.

The region was originally settled in the land rush of the 1890s. The first owners of the Seven D were working ranchers Dewey and Elsie Riddle. They took in guests to supplement their income, launching their dude ranch in the 1920s.

SLEEPING HOUSE (*below*), built of native timber, is where ranch hands once bunked and guests now stay.

For the present ranch owner, Marshall Dominick, the Seven D is a family tradition that began when his father bought the property in 1958. "We love the wilderness surrounding us here," says Marshall, who grew up in Cody, Wyoming. "The only lights we have to contend with at night are the stars in the sky."

PONY-DECALED ARMCHAIR (*right*), draped with faded Indian blanket, is home off the range to the saddle-weary cowboy.

RUSTIC ROCKER AND PRIMITIVE BED in the sleeping house (*left*) reflect the function-not-frills design of wrangler-made ranch furniture.

SNOWSHOES (*left*), remindful of the winter terrain, decorate the outside of a cabin.

COWHIDE SKINS ON A ROUGH-HEWN DAYBED (*right*) take the chill off the mountain air.

122

Fine Crafting
AT A
Wyoming Ranch

Valley Ranch near Yellowstone Park in Wyoming is one of the oldest guest ranches in the West. It was founded in 1915 by two Princeton graduates, Larry Larom and Winn Brooks (of the Brooks Brothers family), but the land was first homesteaded in 1892 by two easterners cut from a rougher cloth, Jim and "Buckskin Jenny" McLaughlin.

SOD-ROOF COTTON-WOOD CABIN (*left*) is an original homesteader's dwelling from the late 1800s. The natural insulating properties of sod helped cool rooms in the summer and warm them in the winter. Sod-roof construction was introduced to the area by Scandinavian settlers.

BIRDHOUSE (*above*) is a crude synopsis of ranch architecture—locally found materials fashioned into dwellings by cowboy carpenters.

BUCKHORN WITH CANDLES (*left*) occupy center stage on a table draped with an old Navajo blanket. Around the fireplace, this one complete with monogrammed screens, visiting dudes gather to exchange stories about the day's trials and triumphs out on the range.

Since 1969, Dr. Oakleigh Thorne II has owned and operated the place with his wife, Lisa. For Oak it was a real homecoming: During his college summers he had worked at the ranch and become a close friend and later a frequent guest of Larom. "He created a simple rustic atmosphere here that had an immediate charm," says Dr. Thorne. Larom also had the good judgment to acquire ranch furniture made by Wyoming native Thomas Molesworth in the 1920s and 1930s, and a collection of pottery, baskets, and blankets.

"Walking onto the ranch is like turning back the clock," Thorne observes. "It's the same feeling you get when you enter an old club in New York City or stop at a New England inn. There's the sensation of time standing still."

Authentic ranch chairs from the 1920s and 1930s suggest the wide range of work done by Cody, Wyoming, craftsman Thomas Molesworth. His rustic creations, using swollen burled fir, tanned and colored leathers, Chimayo New Mexican textiles, and brass tacks to effect a choncha look, are synonymous with western ranch style.

SHADES OF COWBOYS AND INDIANS and silhouetted buckaroo (*top left, above left, and above*) keep the western theme in place. Ranch hands turned odd pieces of lumber into rustic overhead fixtures. The profiled cowboy formerly graced the cover of an early western adventure magazine.

127

BISON HEAD (*right*)
dwarfs other trophies in
the wall menagerie of the
main lodge. Rugs and
blankets are mostly
Navajo; pillow slips are
made from smaller rugs
sewn together.

COWBOY CARICATURE
(*above*) lights up an old
lampshade the way Tom
Mix used to light up the
screen during a Saturday
matinee.

NATURAL BENTWOOD CHAIR (*right*), **with cow-hide back and seat, has a fit-for-a-singing-cowboy look.**

DEER-FOOTED CHAIR (*below*) has an uneven slat back and a cowhide seat.

"BOOTED" CHAIR (*below*) has legs of gnarled and knotted pine and fringed leather armrests.

SIMPLE, RUSTIC BENCH (*below*) is covered with tanned and spotted cowhide.

BARREL CHAIR (*above*), encircled with strips of cowhide, is a familiar container recycled into ranch furniture.

ROPE AND RAWHIDE CHAIR (*above*) is a rough-hewn classic.

CURVED-BACK CHAIR (*above*) is gracefully built yet solid as the tree it came from.

REDWOOD COTTAGE AT
BIG SUR

The real-estate agent had warned them: "You can see through the walls and the floors are crumbling." But when William Ernest Brown and Jim Josoff saw the ramshackle cottage, a short, although winding drive to the Pacific, they immediately recognized the beauty in the ruins. "Once we came to the old wooden gates, we knew this was the one for us," says Josoff. He also knew from the signs of neglect that "the housekeeper here did not do windows—or cobwebs," he adds with a laugh.

CENTENNIAL FLAG from 1876 (*far left*) is a family heirloom. The squat piece of pottery on the table is an early 20th-century New Mexican cooking vessel; the smaller pots are by contemporary Pueblo Indian artisans. Rough-hewn beams and wall paneling were shaped with hand tools.

COASTAL COUNTRY HOUSE (*left*) was built in 1934 with redwood cut from the canyons below. The deep eaves keep the house cool and sloping roofs point the way for heavy rain to run off.

BRICKED ENTRANCE COURT (*above*), protected from the wind, serves as an outdoor living space and walkway for the owners' Labs. Hundreds of terra-cotta pots spawn lush year-round color; in-ground plantings would fall prey to pesky gophers.

REDWOOD TABLE (*left*), with metal braces corroded by time, typifies Big Sur furniture.

Situated on two acres high on a ridge, Sur House enjoys spectacular views of the Pacific coastline and the Santa Lucia mountains. It was built in 1934, even before Highway 1 was completed. Redwood for the construction came from nearby canyons; the soil on the site was used for the foundation —a sun-dried mudsill technique common at the time. "There were no roads to get cement trucks up here back then," Josoff explains.

The owners decided to furnish the house with traditional country pieces at least as old as the building itself. Flea markets, garage sales, and antiques shops in the area provided them with sources. "We had to be true to the house. Its rustic character demanded it," Josoff says.

SQUARED REDWOOD ROUNDS (*right*), cross-sections of trees, are used as an outdoor surface.

REDWOOD BENCH strikes a tranquil pose between towering trees.

STONEWARE AND BAS-KETS (*above*) **lend a rural charm to the redwood kitchen aglow with natural light.**

WEATHERED DECK (*far left*), **cantilevered to canyon views, accommodates a hardy collection of succulents taking in the moist Pacific air.**

STONE FIREPLACE in the living room (*left*) **retains its original hand-wrought iron hood. It easily warms three rooms and even once served as the hot-water heater in the house.**

139

RANCH HOUSE
IN THE NAPA VALLEY

A dirt road provided the only access to the property. The house itself was buried under years of neglect. Even its highly prized views of Napa Valley had been lost to the uncontrolled growth of trees, bushes, and vines. But, after four years of searching for the perfect escape, two transplanted New Yorkers

NAPA VALLEY RANCH HOUSE (*above right*), built in the early 1900s, retains its original screened porch and prized grapevines that trail across its front.

ART NOUVEAU SINK AND MIRROR (*right and far right*) make the morning toilette more memorable, especially in a glass-roofed and -walled bathroom. Antique shower heads affixed to the back of the sink and terra-cotta tiles on the floor turn the room into a spacious indoor-outdoor shower stall.

140

TWIG CHAIR (*above*) **is brightened by an Indian weaving.**

ART DECO LIVING-ROOM FURNITURE (*left*) **looks at home in the restored kitchen. Bought for $500, the set has been appraised for eight times that amount.**

BED WITH NATIVE TIMBER LEGS (*right*), **an owner's design, occupies the revamped bunk-house where the original wood-burning stove continues to provide warmth. The comical deer-footed vase on the pine chest was made by Wisconsin Indians.**

CHRIS MEAD

decided to stake their claim to this less-than-perfect ranch house. "It's in the heart of the California wine country, on a secluded mountaintop surrounded by park land," explains one of the owners. And just as important: the house is only an hour's drive from San Francisco, where they both live and work during the week.

Originally, the plan was to tear down the house completely and live in a remodeled barn on the property. Then, the new owners decided there were practical as well as nostalgic benefits to salvaging the dilapi-

dated retreat they had acquired.

The house proved to be a rare example of an indigenous coastal building style. It had been constructed with materials abundant to the area and also with a keen understanding of the Napa Valley climate. "The people who built this place knew a lot about local weather conditions," says the owner, explaining how the site orientation functions as a natural thermostat, cooling the building in the summer and warming it in the winter. "With this house it was best to leave well enough alone."

The house is that rare California creature—a native. It was constructed without exotic materials or ideas "by the same Chinese laborers who carved the roads into the mountains around here," notes one of the owners. He differentiates it from the homes of people who "play to the Mexican and Spanish heritage of the region and build adobes and haciendas or who put up big châteaus in keeping with the wine country surroundings. This is authentic California. It was a modest, unpretentious house in the beginning and that's all we want it to be."

PEELED TREE-LIMB LAMP (*left*) **with galvanized shade and spindle-wood chair is accompanied by a fried-eggs sign that was a $20 roadside find.**

COWHIDE RUGS
(*above*) **and hand-carved
"gator-legged" table
add their own informal
brands to the living
room.**

PEGGED PINE BED
(*left*)**, dressed in pure
white, reveals a crafts-
man's skill in one of the
owners.**

145

Farmhouses

Farmhouses

Expressing the simple virtues of the farming ethic, the typical country house of the West was built with little concern for popular fashion

TEXAS FARMHOUSE (*preceding pages*), built by German settlers in the 1870s, sits in a field of bluebonnets.

PIE SAFE (*left*) from the 1830s has a Sheraton-like crown that indicates the piece was probably of Anglo-Texas crafts-manship. The house is furnished exclusively with 19th-century Texas antiques.

and every concern for providing shelter for farmer, family, and live-stock. Farmhouse styles emerged from building traditions that frontier settlers brought with them.

Whether newcomers from the East or immi-grants from Europe, farmers built the only way they knew how, usually in the form of a folk adaptation of struc-tures typically found in their original homeland. German arrivals in the Southwest, for example, used traditional *fachwerk* techniques to give their

dwellings a distinctive character, which has been preserved to this day in parts of Texas.

COUNTRY HOME FOR
TEXANA ANTIQUES

The area that sur-rounds Brenham, Texas, possesses some of the prettiest farm and ranch land in the rural reaches of the state. This is where Robbie and Lee Cochran found the country property that had everything—that is, except a house. But, through coincidence,

they found sitting on some business property outside of Houston, a circa 1870 country house. It, too, had every-thing: native longleaf pine timber, original cypress shutters, and evi-dence of hand-built construction. And "it was going to be torn down," says Lee about the struc-ture they saved and moved to the country.

HAND-PLANED DAYBED (*below*) in the living room is typical of farm-made furniture. The settee with patch-work pillows is a pre–Civil War piece.

UNWEATHERED BARN-WOOD (*top*) **was used to construct new kitchen cabinets. William Meyer pottery in all shapes and sizes sits on top of the cabinets.**

WILLIAM MEYER POTTERY (*above*) **was made by a Texas potting family from the late 1880s to 1940. Its trademarks are the slip glaze colors of browns, greens, and ocher, and high-placed handles.**

The Cochrans furnished their home exclusively with Texas antiques of the period. "Every piece of furniture we have is documented. Our intention from the beginning was to be authentic," says Lee. Paint colors were carefully researched and details that were missing, like painted fake chair railings, were added to rooms. Their exhaustive homework paid off with some unexpected finds. A pre–Civil War settee is part of their collection as a result of their spotting it sitting in a driveway waiting to be auctioned.

RABBIT-EARED CHAIRS (*right*) **and an old kitchen worktable furnish the dining room. The use of more than one color of paint is a typical period detail. Here the walls are green; the ceiling, blue; the baseboard, wheat; and a fake chair rail, brown.**

SPOOL BED WITH ACORN FINIALS (*left*), in the children's room, is vintage 1870s to 1880s. Wooden nails that farmers improvised were used to construct the pair of twin beds. The braided rug is from New Hampshire. Basketful of quilts displays midwestern handiwork dating from the 1890s to the 1930s.

SCALLOP-TRIMMED BEDS (*above*), made from abundant pine, illustrate the popular decorative motif favored by Texas craftsmen. The wall-hung quilt is from the 1880s. Texas-made quilts are rare because Texas women, who played as active a role as men in settling the area, had less time than their eastern counterparts to join bees.

"We love the feeling of the house we've created. I only wish the furniture could talk," says Lee, whose insatiable collector's curiosity about the past is well matched to her husband's fifth-generation enthusiasm for Texana. The children also appreciate their house's Texas heritage. "They wanted to know if Daddy had won the 'action' when everybody clapped after we successfully bid on the settee," laughs Lee.

153

FOUR-POSTER PINE BED (*left*) is a new piece made out of old Texas wood. An authentic reproduction, down to its wooden pegs, it was scaled up in size for today's taller Texans. An eight-star quilt occupies a place of honor above the bed.

CARVED SCROLLS in a pine bed, circa 1860 (*above left and left*), display the uncommon talents of an early craftsman. Above the guest room mantel is a rocking horse hooked rug.

EARLY TEXAS DAYBED (*below*), with its graceful Biedermeier lines, is a prized piece.

CHRIS MEAD

VINTAGE ALSATIAN HOUSE IN TEXAS

STEEP-ROOF COUNTRY COTTAGE (*left*), painted adobe red, is typical of the houses built by Alsatian immigrants when they arrived in Texas beginning in 1844.

"Livable Period House" were the watchwords for Tom Messer and Fred Pottinger when they began shopping for an appropriate setting in which to house their remarkable collection of 19th-century Texana.

The 1849 Alsatian cottage they discovered in Castroville, Texas, was the perfect choice—a charming hybrid of French, German, and early Texas styles. The cottage provided them with the authentic background they sought, even though it hardly looked authentic when they first saw it. Six fireplaces had been blocked up and the front porch converted into two bathrooms and a bedroom. "We spent two years just undoing what the previous owners had done," says Pottinger.

MORTAR-FREE STONE WALL (*below*), a Texas German trademark, frames an abundant herb garden.

Each room in the house was appointed to document life as early Texans saw and lived it. So accurate is the restored kitchen that it contains no modern conveniences at all. "We didn't bother to put a real kitchen in the house," says Pottinger. "There's a good restaurant behind us and that's kitchen enough."

IRON FOOD WARMER (*left*) sits in front of the hearth in this 1849 kitchen with original limestone walls. On the mantel are cooking tools collected from the area. The simple cupboard and the Meyer pottery, circa 1870, displayed on the shelves are Texas-made furnishings.

KITCHEN WORKTABLE (*right*), crowded with common cooking paraphernalia of the mid-19th century, sports original blue paint that was a popular color of the time. Prized for its delicate curves, the ash chair has a deerskin seat. The lantern once illuminated a country store.

The sensitivity with which the owners brought this building back to its original style extended to buying a house of similar age in nearby New Braunfels, Texas, just for salvaging authentic materials. Original windows and doors were found abandoned in the barn. Castroville remains the only Alsatian settlement in the United States. Although the craftsmanship is not considered as distinguished as the work of earlier German settlers, the house styles are marked by charm and character that is clearly more French than southwestern.

SAN ANTONIO PINE CUPBOARD (*right*), circa 1850, which dominates the dining room, is considered unusual for its large size. "It's the only one like it I've ever seen," says Texana expert Pottinger. Early Texans used whatever was abundant to construct furniture: A split log became a bench; cowhide for ladderback chair seats. The Pennsylvania table retains traces of its original buttermilk blue paint.

KENTUCKY WEAVER'S CHAIR (*left*), facing a hearth in the dining room, sits next to an old butter churn. On the floor is a braided rug dating from the 1880s, which was made in Castroville.

TURKEY RED TEXAS EMPIRE SOFA (*above*) illustrates the high level the furniture craft reached in the 1860s. The circa 1790 New England baker's table, in front of an antique French grandfather's clock, is the oldest piece in the house.

PECKY CYPRESS TABLE (*right*), with elegant curved legs by a local craftsman, is set for an evening of divertissement before the fire.

BLUE BOW-LEGGED TABLE (*right*) is circa 1860 and made from cypress. It reflects the Victorian influence on Texas furniture-making. Four-poster bed, circa 1850, displays traditional Texas curves. Simple cupboards, such as the blue one here, were household fixtures for storing clothes.

162

From flea market shopping grew a collection that became A Horse of a Different Color, the antiques store that Messer and Pottinger opened in 1962. It quickly turned into the favorite haunt of serious Texana collectors such as the late Ima Hogg of Houston, whose Winedale and Round Top restoration are period museums. "Texas primitive furniture is every bit as good as early New England furniture," notes Pottinger "the only difference is that the craftsmen arrived here a hundred years later."

HORN HAT RACK (*above*) **makes its point. Horn decoration was very popular in Texas ranching communities in the 1860s.**

TEXAS PRIMITIVE BENCH (*left*) **accommodates a new goose decoy by Texas artisan Dave Davis and an old Navajo blanket. The contemporary western painting is by Barry Mullins.**

WOODEN BIRDS (*above right*) by artist James Middleton nest among Texas pottery on a Texas pine cupboard.

COLLECTION IN CUPBOARD (*right, center right, and far right*) includes Texas pine pie safe with punched tin design, originally bought for $20; Mexican cypress cupboard used as a bar; and San Antonio pie safe with punched tin flower and star designs.

TEXAS HILL COUNTRY
HOUSE
★
FOR A
President's Family

Sunset House, near the Lyndon Baines Johnson Ranch in the Texas Hill Country, is where the former First Lady and her family and friends come to enjoy the restorative pleasures of the country: watching the deer graze, hearing the wind rattle in the live oaks, and taking in the spectacle of bluebonnets in the spring (the propagation of wild flowers having been one of the major goals in Lady Bird's beautification program). And, moreover, there are the legendary Texas sunsets to be enjoyed from the shady comfort of the roomy front porch.

GERMAN TEXAS FARMHOUSE (*right*), from the 1890s, welcomes a group of long-legged visitors, who help themselves to Mrs. Johnson's wild flowers.

TEXAS STAR (*below*), the ubiquitous state symbol, twinkles on an iron bench from a train station in Cotulla, Texas.

HAND-STENCILED SCALLOP design (*left*), embellishing the living room, was the traditional method for dressing up plain farmhouse walls. Wicker furniture is in keeping with the informality of the retreat.

TEXAS HALL TREE (*left*) is from President Johnson's childhood home. Making an unscheduled stop on the windowsill is a miniature stagecoach.

MULE DEER CHAIRS (*far left*) around the zinc-topped dining-room table are named for the animal hide that forms their seats.

169

The farmhouse has a quality that is rare these days. "The local stone-work looks as though each rock was hand cut. Even the mortar appears natural in the way it spills over the rocks," says Patsy Stedes, who assisted Mrs. Johnson on the project. Traditional details added by contemporary Texas artisans—stenciling, grain painting, wrought-iron work, and tile decoration—enrich the house in the same manner as the unsung craftsmen who worked on the building before them.

LIMESTONE WALLS (*left*) are the product of local craftsmanship and a thoughtful renovation by Austin architect Roy White. The andirons were made by local blacksmith Lee Weigl, who learned his trade in a WPA program. Over the fireplace is a German inscription.

ANTIQUE STAR QUILT (*below*) covers an ornate high-back Victorian bed of walnut veneer.

3

West in the East

The railroad once carried products and values of eastern society to a West hungry for styles of the "civilized" world. The reverse is true today as objects that capture the rugged character and native expression of the frontier are being brought to cities and suburbs throughout the country.

Vestiges of ranch life such as saddles, chaps, and boots are likely to be transplanted to a New York condominium or a tract house in a bedroom community in the Midwest. Curios made by Indians for the early tourist trade are proudly displayed in private collections that signify, then as now, a desire to bring home a part of the West.

TENNESSEE TWIG CHAIRS encourage stargazing from this Manhattan terrace (*preceding pages*). Potted plants and flowers in handcrafted cedar planters help create a country garden in the city. Stonewashed denim and ticking stripe fabrics are by Ralph Lauren.

NAVAJO CHIEF'S BLANKET (*left*), a treasured antique, commands center stage hanging from the living-room balcony. On the sofa is a blanket of Indian design, an example of the trading post line once manufactured by the American mill, Pendleton.

ENGLISH WINDSOR CHAIR, New England workbench, and rocker (*below*), from the 1800s, provide a rustic yet functional counterpoint to contemporary furniture. In front of the fireplace is a rug with a bold Navajo design expressed in a field of Indian red.

WESTERN DISPLAY IN MANHATTAN
DUPLEX

In the middle of Manhattan, Buffy Birrittella has cultivated a little bit of country for herself. "I'd love to live in a log cabin," she admits, "but

SAWBUCK TABLE (*below*), an 1800s piece from New England, and pre-1800s chairs, still bearing traces of their original apple-green paint, are among the farmhouse furniture.

COUNTRY BASKETS AND POTS OF HERBS (*far left*) **add farmhouse flair to a well-organized kitchen.**

SANTA FE FASHIONS (*top left*)**, a sweater by Ralph Lauren and a handwoven Indian jacket, hang companionably from a wooden peg rack; a northeastern Indian basket finds its niche.**

NEW ENGLAND DRY SINK (*center left*)**, from the 1800s, and an old Navajo rug are paired with a tall cactus. On top of the sink is a Hopi pot.**

WOODEN PEG RACK (*bottom left*) **is hung with ethnic jewelry as well as towels.**

that's pretty impossible when I have to work in the city." So, she did the next best thing and gathered her collection of country Americana and native crafts around her in an elegant roost.

Here, in the wide-open spaces of her duplex apartment, East meets West in a fusion of primitive styles and modern architecture. "I wanted the space to be as gallery-like as possible," she explains, "to draw attention to the craftsmanship of each piece."

As a collector, Buffy first trained her eye on the shapes and textures of New England Indian baskets because "you can see the craft of each maker."

Buffy's collection of southwestern Indian rugs, blankets, and pottery grew in her travels as a vice-president with the Ralph Lauren organization. Her enchantment with the West dates from a visit to a friend's ranch in Utah. "I couldn't get over the incredible sense of space and the freedom it brings," she says. "I like to think I have some of it here."

WESTERN BLANKETS
(left), **factory-made by Pendleton Mills and Beacon Mills between 1900 and 1950, are now considered collector's items. The Pendleton wool blankets on the rattan furniture are woven with reversible Indian designs.**

DIAMOND-PANED WINDOWS *(right)*, **with original wood mullions, provide a 19th-century view of the outdoors. Reflecting the tastes of the owners, art and photography books share the table with a western skull in a wooden bowl.**

INDIAN PATTERNS FOR A

In summer, the trails of sand and wet towels are dead giveaways that the ocean is nearby. But the Indian-patterned blankets, hung trading-post style from the upstairs balcony, suggest a comfortable cabin out west rather than a 19th-century carriage house on the Long Island shore.

Celebrated fashion photographer Bruce Weber and Nan Bush share this house with their two cats, their dog Rowdy, and an unusual collection of American-made blankets. With the imaginative visual sense that distinguishes photographs of clothing by Ralph Lauren, Calvin Klein, and Perry Ellis, Weber recognized the original design in numerous blankets once considered throwaways because they had been made in a mill.

"Many Indians used their own handwoven blankets to trade with and bought the mill-

GAZEBO GUEST QUARTERS (*below*), handmade by artist friend John Ryman, provide an offbeat and comfortable place to sleep on a summer weekend. Railings are crafted from twisted tree limbs.

SHIPWRECK-SALVAGED WALLS (*right*) were pieced together from a cargo of doors found in a sunken vessel. The mantel of the painted white brick fireplace exhibits favorite old photographs.

CAMP COLORS (*below*) dominate a pair of Beacon blankets.

made blankets for themselves," explains Michael Malce, whose Manhattan store, Kelter-Malce, specializes in this unique Americana. Some of these blankets became the favorite bunk covering at summer camps throughout the country in the first half of this century.

Such blankets are an appropriate complement to the warmth and authenticity of this special residence. "We really haven't touched the inside of the house at all," Nan says, "except to sweep out the birds' nests when we moved in."

FRONTIER OUTPOST
ON LONG ISLAND

"Growing up in England, we all had this fascination about the West," says Chris Mead, a New York–based photographer. "I was completely enthralled with cowboys and Indians and western stars like Roy Rogers and John Wayne as a kid." Once he planted his feet in the real West for the first time, the Briton became a native. Nowadays, the only shoes he wears are cowboy boots, which he collects with a passion, and his cottage on Long Island could easily be mistaken for an outpost on the frontier, albeit a sophisticated one.

CHICAGO RODEO BANNER (*left*), from the 1920s, and collections of well-worn boots and Indian blankets are among the cabin's authentic reminders of sunsets in the West.

COWBOY CABIN (*right*) is a summer retreat from city canyons.

183

BANDANNA NAPKINS, an Indian blanket, and a tin coffeepot (*above*) add western touches to a seaside table.

PLAINS OF THE EAST (*right*), seen through the kitchen windows, are set off by the ocean instead of mountains.

184

TEXAS LADDER-BACK (*above*) **with cowhide seats hangs Shaker style from the ceiling.**
NATURAL WHITE CANVAS (*left*) **takes a southwestern turn, disguising a pair of twin beds as sofas in a softer imitation of whitewashed adobe.**
COUNTRY BASKET (*below*), **embellished by an Indian design, erupts with a profusion of baby's breath.**

185

Log Cabin

NEAR THE NATION'S CAPITAL

Before Nancy Clark Reynolds moved into her Arlington, Virginia, log cabin home, a miniature cabin collection was her only means for indulging in a lifelong fantasy. "Ever since I was a little girl growing up on the family ranch in Idaho," she says, "I've wanted to live in a log cabin." A busy and successful career as a Washington, D.C., lobbyist seemed to rule out the possibility of achieving that dream. "Then one day a friend called and said he had found my house," Nancy reports. It turned out to be an authentic log cabin no more than ten minutes from downtown Washington.

VIRGINIA LOG CABIN (*left*) brings the Sawtooth Mountains of Idaho closer to home in the suburbs for Washington, D.C., lobbyist Nancy Clark Reynolds.

WILD WEST WREATH (*above*), made of grapevine, is hung with miniature cowboy boots, tiny clay burros-of-burden, and egg-shaped ornaments hand-painted by a young Navajo boy.

WESTERN GEAR (*above*) hangs from pegs on the front porch.

KEROSENE LANTERN (*left*) from the original Reynolds family ranch lights up the front porch. The brass bell once announced visitors to a friend's country antiques shop. The carved horse prancing on the rafter, tail and mane of tin, originally decorated an Idaho barn.

187

Nancy Reynolds's childhood home in Idaho was a ranch originally homesteaded by a great-uncle around the turn of the century. It is located in what Nancy unabashedly calls "the most beautiful place on earth"—a valley in the Alpine setting of the Sawtooth Mountains. Her cabin in suburban Virginia is filled with reminders of growing up in the West. Branding irons, ranch-house lanterns, stirrups, even a tin tub where she took baths as a child, made the trip East with her. "I kept thinking one day I'd have a log cabin to put all these things in," she says, "and now I do."

DENIM-COVERED FURNITURE (*left*) and bold Indian art immediately call to mind the West. The painting, *Olla Bearer,* is by American Indian artist John Nieto (see page 39). The primitive pine side table in the foreground came out of a sheep wagon like those that once roamed the Pyrenees of France and the valleys of Idaho.

FAMILY HOMESTEAD (*above*), well documented with early photos, was called Robinson Bar Ranch after the prospector who once panned for gold in a stream running through the property.

STONE HEARTH (*left*) is decked with vestiges of the frontier, including branding irons that bear the family stamp, southwestern pottery, and ranch-house graniteware. The sled, a heart's delight, is a Virginia antique.

189

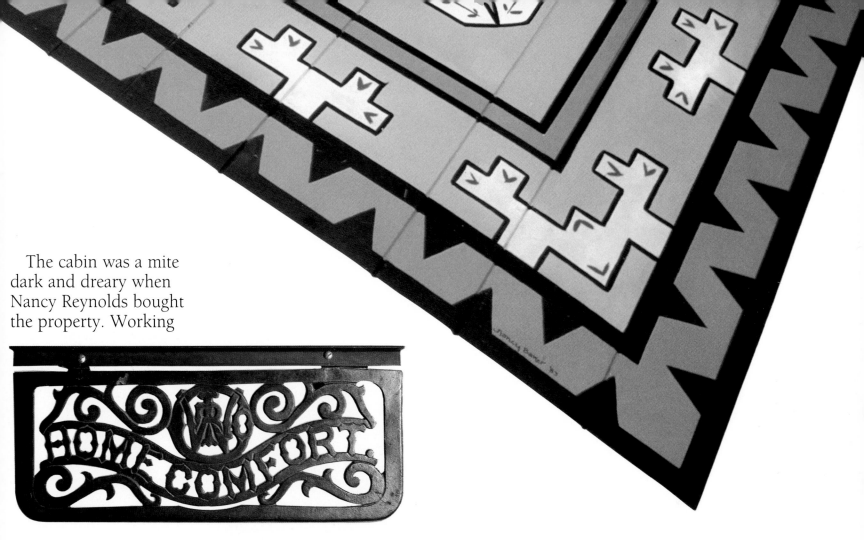

The cabin was a mite dark and dreary when Nancy Reynolds bought the property. Working with architectural designer Bill Austin, she added skylights and windows to improve views of an acre full of century-old trees. "Every window makes a beautiful picture," she says, "and whenever I look out at the big pine tree in my yard, it brings me home to Idaho."

NAMEPLATE FROM OLD STOVE (*above*) sums up the owner's feelings about hearth and home.

PAINTED FLOOR (*far left and above*), resembling a Navajo rug, is a western interpretation of a folk art practice by artist Nancy Baker. An upside-down bedpost provides the improbable axis for a surprisingly elegant hand-fashioned dining-room chandelier. The wreath festooned with spirit dolls is from Señora Valdez's Christmas Market in Santa Fe.

191

LOG CABIN MASTER BEDROOM is reminiscent of the owner's childhood home, with the soft colors of the Idaho-made quilts, pillows, curtains, and upholstery fabrics.

Although the hills of Arlington are a far cry from Nancy Reynolds's beloved Sawtooth Mountains, the road here, nonetheless, leads to home. "Whenever I turn into my driveway and see this cabin, my heart leaps," she declares. The house, constructed by previous owners from a New England Log Home kit, is a dwelling unique to this bedroom community—a westerner's refuge in the middle of suburban Virginia.

SCREENED PORCH (*left*) holds the miscellany of ranch life: stirrups, iron gate fixtures, a barrel hoop, lanterns, hinges, and kitchen gadgets. The primitive wood carving of the Spanish coat of arms (*foreground*) originally came from Guatemala. The log cabins are some of the miniatures the owner once collected as a substitute for living in the real thing.

CANVAS-COVERED SHEEP WAGON from Idaho (*above*) pulled into the owner's Virginia property one Christmas morning as a surprise from family and friends.

4

Cowboy and Indian Crafts

The heritage of the American West is in the hands of artists and craftsmen who practice their skills with the same enthusiasm and fidelity to detail as their forebears of hundreds and even thousands of years ago. Today, dedicated cowboy artisans carry on trades like saddlemaking and ropemaking that were so important in the taming of the frontier a century ago. Chimayo weavers of New Mexico work at their looms using the same approach introduced to the New World by the Spanish in the 17th century. Indian basketmakers employ the painstaking techniques perfected by their ancestors centuries before.

Whether pursuing their crafts in a historic

BRANDING IRONS (*preceding pages*) are Slim Green's mementos of his days as a cowboy.

SADDLEMAKER SLIM GREEN (*left*) poses with his art. The woven basket design in the center is his interpretation of an old western style.

pueblo in the desert or a contemporary studio in town, western craftsmen share in common a deeply felt pride in their work, as well as a commitment to teaching the

SILVER SADDLEHORN CAP (*above*) displays a master craftsman's remarkable silverwork.

traditions of their discipline to new generations. The output of these individuals ranges from practical necessities such as riding tack and house furnishings to the more

elegant statements found in silver belts or Indian pottery. These various crafts, taken together, are an accurate expression of the multifaceted western experience.

Austin "Slim" Green likes to recall the advice of Pop Bettis, a legendary Lubbock, Texas, saddlemaker who taught Green his craft: "Soon as you think you've got a saddle perfect, you might as well crawl into the casket." Since 1934, Slim has been perfecting saddles that his customers consider works of art.

"I make every saddle for the person who's going to ride it," Slim says. The "tree," or saddle foundation, carved out of lodgepole pine and covered with heavy rawhide, is made to order for each customer to guarantee a perfect fit for both rider and horse. He builds up the seat with layers of leather, shaving the layers as he goes with a shaving tool.

Green has the tannery select leather from range-grazed steers, which he considers better than feedlot-cattle hides. He leaves his most distinguishable mark in the

199

designs he tools from memory into the leather. After soaking the leather in water, Slim carves the outline of the desired figure, then hammers in its detail with metal stamps of his own creation. After the saddle has been dried, oiled, and polished, it is ready to serve on the horse's back as an original western artwork.

Slim Green has been both a working and a rodeoing cowboy, and his horse- and leather-sense have made him one of the undisputed saddle kings of New Mexico. "People know I can ride the saddles I make, even though I won't bounce as good as I used to."

Now semiretired, he is still visited by people looking for saddles of rare quality, such as the Indian-blanket type that is his proudest creation. It is tooled with such precision that it looks as though a horse wearing this saddle is really wearing a blanket.

"Make something good, but try to be a little bit different" is another Popism that has served Slim Green well.

TOOLS OF SLIM'S TRADE (*right*), used to assemble saddles, line a backboard in his Tesuque, New Mexico, workshop.

LEATHER CUPS (*below*) reveal Slim's precision freehand art and contain the tools he uses to carve flowers, leaves, fighting stallions, and western vistas into leather. Many of his tools are hand-me-downs from old-timers who crafted leather in the early 1900s; others are by Slim himself.

In his Longhorn Saddle Shop in the outskirts of Laramie, Wyoming, Andy Hysong hand-crafts western tack in the traditional manner learned the traditional way. He apprenticed with an old-timer, beginning by sweeping floors and performing menial tasks around the shop. Leathercrafting and saddlemaking were taught to him over five years.

Hysong still takes no shortcuts when turning hides into saddles and metal into spurs. A fancy saddle, from construction of the ground seat (or "tree") to tooling of the design, takes as much as three weeks to complete. At least a week is required to make a pair of spurs. Hysong forges his own steel and engraves patterns into silver overlays. It's a tedious process, but the craftsman doesn't mind. "I love what I do and always have," he says.

WESTERN TACK (*above left*) by Andy Hysong is made with a cowboy-craftsman's understanding of a saddle's function.

SPURS (*right*) display the craftman's versatility. Rowels—the business end of a spur—are the star and sawtooth spiked wheels shaped to suit a rider's needs. Just as roping and bull riding require different skills, they also demand different spurs.

202

Silversmithing

Bill Bell is a Texas rancher who makes belts, buckles, and bracelets according to techniques he learned from the southwestern Indians. For his larger pieces, he pours ingots himself, then hammers them into sheet silver. For smaller pieces, he pounds an old silver coin until it is smooth, just as the metal-scarce Indians of an earlier era did. Next, using a hammer-and-punch technique, Bell transfers his meticulous stampwork onto the silver.

COINS HAMMERED INTO CONCHAS (*right and below*) and sheet silver punched with Bill Bell's inimitable stampwork transform the craftsman's western belts into collector's items.

SWIVEL KNIFE ARTIST Clint Fay (*left*) stands outside his Wyoming studio.

The art of leather tooling as displayed by Clint Fay is what turns standard western gear into wearable western art. His unique stamp—the freehand designs he pounds into wet leather—is the result of learning by doing. But it is his swivel knife, an instrument manipulated by thumb and middle finger while pressure is maintained by still another digit, that turns the designs into tooled western relief. From such dexterity comes the carved patterns, intricate florals, and fancy letters of a distinctive western art form.

INTRICATE PRECISION TOOLING (*below and far left*) on belts and holsters is the leather craftsman's personal imprint. Fay pounds, cuts, and chisels his freehand designs into leather.

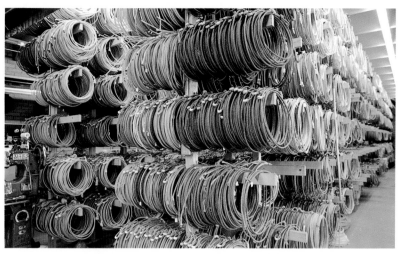

Ropemaking

Next to his horse and saddle, a cowboy's best friend is his rope. Don King's Saddlery and Ropes in Sheridan, Wyoming, sells more than 40,000 lengths of rope a year to ranching and rodeoing cowboys. Hand-twisted nylon and polyester are by far the most popular material—they are more durable and less expensive than natural fibers. But King's Ropes also continues to stretch and tie Portuguese sisal lariats, for riders who prefer the feel of this material. "A cowboy may go through a hundred ropes until he finds the one that's right for him," King explains.

HAND-COILED ROPES (*above*), prestretched for the working cowboy, are ready for immediate use.

ROPE STRETCHING (*left*) at the King ranch entails a three-week operation just to take the curl out of the coil.

LARIATS OF CHOICE (*below*) for the professional rodeo rider are Portuguese sisal.

CHRIS MEAD

BRONZE CASTING

Wyoming artist Skip Glomb relies on his years spent as a wrangler, rodeo rider, and hunting guide to bring hunks of clay and wax to life with the realism that only a cowboy knows by heart. Sometimes dozens of casts are discarded before the final, precise mold is struck. It is only then that Glomb delivers his piece to the Montana foundry he uses for the actual casting.

Glomb's rugged hands are the tools that mold, shape, and sculpt his western experience. Although equipped with a studio at his ranch, Glomb does his hardest work while rounding up cattle, fishing, or puttering around in the corral. "I complete everything in my mind before I even begin," Glomb says.

COWBOY-TURNED-WESTERN-ARTIST Glomb (*left*) is shown in the studio that is his home away from home on the range.

LIFELIKE BRONZE PORTRAITS (*left*) are Skip Glomb's evocation of the cowboy West. His gift for rendering detail comes from years of experience as a working cowboy.

CHRIS MEAD

209

THE Santa Fe INDIAN MARKET

The Santa Fe Indian Market, a yearly event, attracts native American artists and craftspeople from throughout the Southwest and numerous collectors as well. The wares on display, though newly made, perpetuate the Indians' ancient tradition of artistic expression, making their work our most enduring American heritage.

CEREMONIAL DRESS (*right*) of a southwestern tribeswoman is a dramatic example of the American Indian's talent for transforming ordinary materials like buckskin, beads, and feathers into stately raiments.

HANDWOVEN BASKETS (*above and left*) are coveted market buys. Fewer than a dozen baskets may represent the weaver's entire output for a year.

POTTERY
Native Clay

As she digs up the New Mexican clay that is the medium of her art, Priscilla Hoback can "feel the history of the land, its rawness and beauty." At the potter's wheel her strong hands give the clay shape and function.

But it is the manner in which she paints her color glazes onto pots, bowls, platters, and plates that supplies the work with its distinctive character, one clearly influenced by her study of the techniques of Japanese, Chinese, and Korean potters.

With the deftness of a Sumi painter, she brushes on layers of glaze which, when fired in the kiln, produce bold abstractions of the southwestern landscape she knows so well. Says the artist, "I shape my work from the environment— the feel, texture, and variation of my native land."

NATIVE CLAY POTS (*left and below*), born of the historic New Mexican earth, are the work of artist Priscilla Hoback, who lives in Galisteo, New Mexico.

PAINTED GLAZES (*bottom*) are at once Oriental, derived from Sumi painting, and New Mexican, colored by the richly hued landscape.

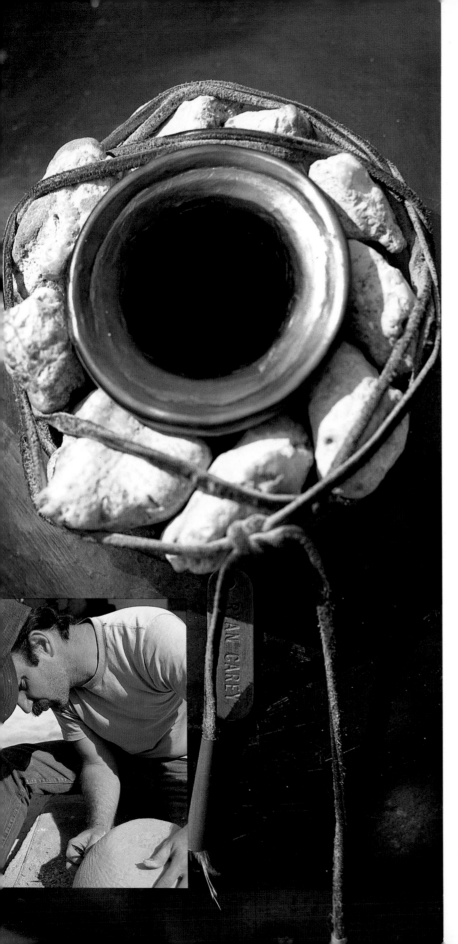

POTTERY
ORIGINAL PLASTER

From the flotsam and jetsam of metal, glass, wood, rope, leather, beads, textiles, and animal bones, constructivist artist Ryan Carey imprints the historic and contemporary Southwest onto recycled pots or, more often, his own uniquely formed vessels. These vessels are not the product of the potter's wheel but rather are sculpted in a colored "eggshell plaster" of the artist's own making and then treated with applications of heat, acid, and carving to obtain the desired texture. To complete the sculpture, Carey affixes often surprising materials that he has collected.

"It's always surprising to discover in a contemporary work such historical awareness," says Mac McLean, director of Artefacts, the Los Angeles gallery that exhibits Carey's work. Using native materials such as turquoise, river rock, and cactus needles, Carey creates a Southwest that is both familiar and original.

RAW CHUNKS OF TURQUOISE (*left*) **rim a black Oaxacan polished stone vessel bound with rawhide. The construction measures 21 inches wide and 10 inches high.**

CONTEMPORARY CALIFORNIA artist Ryan Carey (*left*) **studied classical sculpture before developing his unique methods for synthesizing the familiar elements of the American Southwest.**

CONSTRUCTIONS (*opposite page, clockwise from top left*)**: eggshell plaster with saddle blanket remnant; cactus-spined vessel; river rock and geometric sgraffito design; incised design of pink paint over gray stoneware crock; terra-cotta vessel with aged pink finish; turquoise-colored finish with stone metate and feather detail; rubber fish wedged between turquoise and river rock; and pre-Columbian parrotmen figures on burnished ceremonial vessel.**

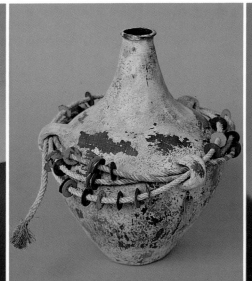

BOBBIN AND SHUTTLE (*left*) are threaded with yarn, which will be woven into a garment or floor covering.

WEAVING
ORTEGA FAMILY

The small, rural town of Chimayo, New Mexico, has a centuries-old tradition of weaving. "The Spanish brought sheep raising and the art of the loom to New Mexico in the 1600s," explains David Ortega, whose family has been weaving for seven generations in a style that remains virtually unchanged. As children, he and his siblings were given the chore of winding the yarn onto spools for the weavers. It was only

AT THE LOOM (*left*), David Ortega continues the family weaving tradition begun by Gabriel de Ortega in the 1700s.

natural that they move on to the loom. Unlike comparable Indian work, Chimayo weavings feature "spotted or scattered patterns," according to Ortega, "rather than one overall design."

"The craft grew out of necessity," explains David. "Garments and blankets were woven for warmth." Even today, Chimayo weavings are bought as much for their practical value as their beauty.

CHIMAYO WEAVINGS (*below*) are also called Rio Grande weavings after the river that crosses the state. The pattern of concentric multicolored diamonds on a serape is considered the pinnacle of Chimayo craft. The town became such a productive weaving center that its name is now used as a generic term for New Mexican textiles.

Weaving
TRUJILLO FAMILY

The Trujillo recipe for making natural dyes has been in this family of master weavers ever since their Spanish New Mexican ancestors first crushed native southwestern flowers, berries, nuts, vegetables, and even insects to color their wool yarn. Today, Jacobo Trujillo, the seventy-six-year-old patriarch of the family, continues to work on the loom he built in 1927.

His wife, Isabelle, still hand-cards and spins fleece into yarn for the dozen or so pieces he will weave a year.

"My father had five brothers but he is the only one who is still weaving," says son Irvin, the seventh generation of Trujillos to carry on this tradition. Although they no longer raise their own sheep for wool, members of the family still use the Spanish colonial designs and many of the original techniques at the studios on their ranch in the foothills above Chimayo, New Mexico.

In addition to weaving such traditional textiles as blankets, *jerga* floor coverings, and *sabanilla* sheeting and clothing, family members also practice the woodworking crafts of colonial New Mexico, carving religious figures and making furniture out of local wood. "My sister weaves and paints retablos, her husband is a master carver, and my wife is an accomplished weaver," Irvin notes. "This is our way of keeping the traditions of our colonial heritage alive."

SKEINS OF NATURALLY DYED WOOL (*above*) provide the unique colors of the authentic colonial weavings made by the Trujillos at their Centinela Traditional Arts studio in New Mexico.

HARNESS LOOM (*left*), a colonial New Mexican fixture, is operated by Irvin Trujillo to weave designs that date from the 17th century. The new loom was handbuilt by Irvin's brother-in-law, Marco Oviedo.

219

Furniture-Making
RANCH STYLE

"It had been around so long, we hated to see it not being built," says Stan Hopper about the furniture he creates using the designs and techniques of Thomas Molesworth. "We're making pieces the way Molesworth did in the 1920s," using the same bulbous fir common to Wyoming in combination with straight fir poles, hardwoods, leather, and Chimayo upholstery.

The techniques of peeling, sanding, and storing the wood were passed along to the Hoppers when they purchased the Wyoming Furniture Company from Molesworth's apprentice, Paul Hindman, who had continued the designs over the years, adding some of his own adaptations along the way.

The Molesworth "look" began with a chance commission. A woman asked the young woodworker if he could make a bed for her out of some large

pieces of gnarled wood she had come upon while hiking. The bed that resulted established a new western style and marked the start of Molesworth's successful furniture-making career.

Today, the Hopper family continues in the Molesworth tradition, even traveling by horseback into the Cody high country to bring back the coveted knotted fir limbs. Says Hopper, "We're just trying to keep things as authentic as possible."

BULBOUS FIR LOGS (*left*), soon to provide the legs for a chair or sofa, are prepared by Stan Hopper in his Wyoming workroom.

MOLESWORTH APPRENTICE Paul Hindman (*below*), shown in old newspaper clippings, carried on his mentor's rustic furniture-making traditions for many years.

CARVED SILHOUETTES (*right*) and landscapes routed into wood by Stan Hopper are applied to pieces of furniture as western decoration.

HIGH-BACKED CHAIR (*right*) is upholstered in blue leather with figures of buffalo and trees by Stan Hopper.

KNOTTED FIR TRESTLE TABLE (*top far right*), with pole trim edges, is typical of Molesworth's sturdy designs.

PEELED BEDPOSTS (*center far right*), with lassoed headboard and footboard, have painted decoration by Melody Hopper.

HARDWOOD BED (*bottom far right*), made of magnolia, has fir posts and hand-painted wildlife scenes.

GNARLED LEG POSTS (*right*), on a sofa, and routed wildlife scene are Molesworth trademarks, as are the use of Chimayo weavings to cover cushions and brass conchalike tacks.

TIMBER WITH GNARLS AND KNOTS (*above*) became Molesworth's signature. The peculiarly distorted fir timber is sorted by size and left to dry for three years after being cut down.

222

The colloquial styles of Spanish New Mexico are expressed in the furniture designs of Peter Gould. "My pieces are constructed like those of Spanish craftsmen who used pine or juniper, because that was the only timber available, and who relied on precision joinery.

The personality in his designs, however, is pure Gould, expressed in such whimsy as putting rockers on a mission chair or embellishing pieces with carvings and colors.

Gould lives and works at Quartermill Farm in rural Galisteo, New Mexico, with his potter wife Priscilla Hoback (see page 213). Here, he crafts furniture to be used rather than admired as museum pieces. "I like building a table that delights the senses as art," says Gould, "but also makes you feel good when you lean back in a chair and put your feet up on it."

AZTEC FEATHERS, scalloped fan, and twelve-sided rosette (*above*) on chairbacks reflect the craftsman's proficiency as a wood-carver.

BARN WOOD STOOLS (*left*) are rustic examples of Gould's early work.

19TH-CENTURY WOOL WAREHOUSE (*right*) is where Peter Gould crafts southwestern country furniture. The "Fannie Bell" rockers, his rendering of a Texas mission style, are named in memory of his grandmother. The side chair is Gould's version of an early Spanish New Mexican style.

FURNITURE-MAKING

COLORADO RUSTIC STYLE

Steve Cappellucci is a modern Svengali when it comes to turning raw timber into one-of-a-kind handmade furniture. He learned his craft from his grandfather, David Work, who built log houses and furniture in the Colorado Rockies.

"He handled wood in a rustic way like the craftsmen of the Adirondack movement," says Steve, whose own furniture expresses a similar rugged character with more refinement.

Working with the peculiarities of timber native to Colorado, and using such precision joinery as pegging, dovetailing, and mortise-and-tenon, Cappellucci has produced log chairs, tables, and benches—many of them shown in the house appearing on pages 92–101—that look like they were plucked from the nearby forest.

Steve mastered his craft after thousands of hours of effort. "When I came to work for Dave, I didn't know anything about furniture building," he admits. "I liked Dave's ideas of using native materials; it was a good excuse to get outdoors. And I enjoyed the challenge of working with irregular shapes."

WORKSHOP BUILT BY HAND (*left*) combines partially hand-peeled logs with smooth-milled timber. Steve Cappellucci is the craftsman who uses oddly shaped timber for furniture and architectural details.

WESTERN WINDSOR BENCH (*below*) shows the craftsman's technique for turning lodgepole pine into artful furniture.

227

In the twisted forms of nature, Cappellucci finds the raw material for his designs. He cuts, peels, sands, and oils the odd timber pieces to bring out the natural grain and color of the wood, then painstakingly joins them. The result is unique country furniture as much the product of a woodsman's eye as the craftsman's hands.

BARREL CHAIR (*far right*) is made in the rugged style perfected by David Work, Cappellucci's grandfather.

CAPPELLUCCI CURVE (*above right*) in the arm of the chair is actually four pieces of wood crafted together.

228

TWISTED LAMP BASE (*right*) supports shade of aspen wood slats laced with leather strips.

RUSTIC ROCKER (*far left*) displays elegant mortise-and-tenon curves; seat and back are of hand-woven leather.

BABY'S HIGH CHAIR (*left*) is an early Cappellucci design.

LODGEPOLE PINE CHAIR (*below*) required thirty hours to build, excluding time for preliminary drying.

Furniture-Making

IDAHO RUSTIC STYLE

Dean Beaudet will spend hours at the sawmill looking through what amounts to a million feet of forest for the right logs to use in his handmade custom furniture. It can take him a week to clean one log and 130 man-hours to build a four-poster bed. "You can't rush through this. You have to stand back and look at what you're doing," says the general contractor turned craftsman.

Beaudet eyes every little knothole, "check" (the natural timber crack), and ring for the textural interest they bring to his

LOG FOUR-POSTER BED (*below*), by Dean Beaudet, is designed around the natural shape and texture of logs, including their knots, blemishes, and cracks.

Natural Woods designs. He dreams of working with a piece of centuries-old timber from the upper reaches of the Idaho mountains. "I'd love to find a sugar pine that is about to go. I'd need a helicopter to get to it," he contemplates, "but I can just imagine the rings."

"CHECKS" IN TIMBER (*left*), as in this sofa arm, are characteristic of Beaudet's rustic works.

RUGGED BEDPOST (*above*), of peeled pine, has white coloration that is achieved by stripping bark from green wood promptly after it has been cut.

231

Although much of the frontier West has been lost to progress, the heritage of the region remains secure in collections that document early western life and in such unspoiled natural refuges as Yellowstone National Park. This remarkable legacy survives only because of individual efforts, including those of early conservationists who made sure that a magnificent chunk of primitive America would remain undeveloped, and a Wyoming couple who kept one small part of the frontier from biting the dust.

On modern cattle ranches and along the thriving rodeo circuit, the western heritage is also alive and well, as cowboys practice skills and perpetuate the customs of the range. Even though the legendary frontier has disappeared, the spirit of the West lives on in the people, places, and events.

Old Trail Town

"We wanted to preserve a part of America's heritage," says Terry Edgar about Old Trail Town, a collection of 19th-century frontier buildings that she and her husband, Bob, have assembled in Cody City, Wyoming. The structures were moved from their original locations

CORTEGE OF FRONTIER WAGONS (*preceding pages*) **parades in Old Trail Town, Wyoming.**

TRADING-POST CABIN (*left*), **where pelts were bartered for whiskey, flour, and ammunition, was built in 1883. Relocated, it serves as home to artist and amateur historian Bob Edgar.**

WAGON WHEEL (*above*) **has made its final stop on the trail.**

ICE AND WATER WAGONS (*left*) **stand beside a saloon dating from 1888.**

MUSEUM OF THE OLD WEST (*left and far left*) **has thoroughly authentic buildings, down to the chinking between logs.**

along an 1880 stage-coach route, then installed on the present site.

The Edgars, who are the sole residents of Trail Town, went to great lengths to preserve a historic era. "We hauled our own coal and water for fourteen years to save up to buy more buildings," Terry says. "They were being lost over the years to the weather, vandals, and neglect. We couldn't stand to see them destroyed." Among the structures saved: a hide-out for the notorious "Hole in the Wall" gang and a cabin used by "Curly," General Custer's chief scout.

The Wyoming natives have high hopes for their restoration project. "The museum will do a lot for people now, but will do even more for the next generation" as the West recedes still further into the past.

WESTERN BENCH (*above*), improvised from tree stumps and a log, is a rough-cast rest stop.

ONE-ROOM SCHOOL-HOUSE (*left*) shows the woodworking skills of its builders, early Scandinavian immigrants.

CATTLEMAN'S CABIN (*top*), constructed in 1879, was the home of Charles Carter, who introduced cattle ranching to the Big Horn Basin. A huge bearskin dominates one wall and a display of early photographs captures the authentic West.

237

PIO PICO MANSION

During the 19th century, California was ruled by three successive flags—Spanish, Mexican, and American. The historic Pio Pico mansion, home of the last governor of Mexican California, exists as a link to the life and times of that turbulent transition period characterized by wars, revolutions, and territorial disputes.

The thirteen-room, two-story mansion was built in 1852 on a site that is now a California state park. Damaged by floods, the house was rebuilt and has twice been restored. It is a repository of period furniture as well as a remarkable example of regional adobe architecture.

STRAIGHT-BACK CHAIRS with rawhide seats (*left*) **exemplify the practical style of California frontier furniture. The Indian blanket was a common table covering in a 19th-century southwestern kitchen. On the table are Indian cooking utensils.**

VICTORIAN ROSE-WOOD BED (*left*) **was a frontier luxury "imported" from back East. An antique Navajo blanket, draped over a leather trunk, provided additional warmth. The ceramic pitcher and washbowl were standard bedside companions in the period predating modern bathrooms.**

ANGLO-INFLUENCED DOOR SURROUND (*left*), **its blue paint bleached pale with time, reflects the building traditions introduced by Yankee emigrants.**

PITCHED ROOF LINE (*bottom left*), **lost when an earlier restoration added a mission gable to the house, was ultimately recovered. The adobe is an amalgam of Mexican, Spanish, and American domestic building styles, all of which influenced architecture in this region.**

The Buffalo Bill
HISTORICAL CENTER
★ ★ ★ ★ ★ ★ ★ ★ ★ ★ ★

Nowhere is the spirit of the West captured more colorfully than in its legendary heroes. "Buffalo Bill" died in 1917 but remains the quintessential American frontiersman. An Indian scout, Pony Express rider, and buffalo hunter *extraordinaire* (with his aptly named "Lucrezia Borgia" rifle, he slew 4,000 head in a single year), William F. Cody converted his plentiful natural talents and gift for the stage into a spectacular traveling exhibition of frontier derring-do. The debut in 1883 of "Buffalo Bill's Wild West" catapulted Cody into fame as Amer-

OLD WESTERN ADVERSARIES (*left and right*), the Indian brave and Indian scout, Colonel Buffalo Bill Cody, make an appearance at the Cody, Wyoming, centennial celebration of "Buffalo Bill's Wild West," which debuted in 1883.

ica's first genuine media star. He toured the United States and Europe with an entourage of 640 cowboys, Indians, Rough Riders, musicians, and technicians, plus more than 400 animals including horses, cattle, and buffalo.

At his death, some 25,000 mourners paid their last respects. The most enduring tribute to Cody, however, is undoubtedly the Buffalo Bill Historical Center in Cody, Wyoming.

One of the four museums here is devoted entirely to Buffalo Bill's personal effects and Wild West Show memorabilia. The Winchester Arms Museum has a collection of over 5,000 firearms. The Plains Indian Museum displays the crafts and traditions of tribes from the area between the Mississippi River and the Rocky Mountains.

The cornerstone of this complex is the Gloria Vanderbilt Whitney Gallery of Western Art, an impressive collection of work by masters of the western genre, including Charles Russell and Frederic Remington.

SCULPTED "SCOUT" (*right*), a likeness of Colonel Cody by Gloria Vanderbilt Whitney, points the way to the Buffalo Bill Historical Center.

242

BUFFALO BILL MUSEUM

REMINGTON'S STUDIO (*left*) in New Rochelle, New York, has been faithfully reconstructed at the Buffalo Bill Historical Center. Remington, one of the foremost chroniclers of the West, created most of his work from this studio, relying on authentic costumes and paraphernalia collected during his visits West.

COWBOY DERRING-DO (*below and below left*) was the soul of the old Wild West show. Trick riders and stagecoach drivers thrill audiences today, as they did then, with displays of their amazing skills.

BUCKSKINNED BUFFALO BILL (*below*) is a modern incarnation of America's first celebrity cowboy.

THE RODEOING WEST

Myth and reality are still alive in the West. The neon buck rider that enlivens a roadside sign is a faithful copy of the rodeo rider who puts it all on the line in an eight-second ride, week after week. Bursting out of the chute astride an ornery bull or bronco, the rodeo cowboy brings the sport and ritual of the West to a packed center ring.

The rodeo grew out of the original cattle drives. After days of working and riding on the range, cowboys looked forward to enjoying one another's company and having some fun. They gathered at the railheads at the end of the drive and, for entertainment, arranged some informal competition designed to test and show off their horsemanship. As the railroad advanced west and more towns sprang up, local residents began to provide an appreciative audience for the cow-

CHRIS MEAD

244

boys and their feats. In 1888, a grandstand was erected for one such occasion in Prescott, Arizona, and a small admission was charged. Thus was born the modern sport of rodeo.

Today, whether it takes place in a small-town arena or a big-city dome, the rodeo is a chance to witness the classic confrontation of cowboy and beast in a duel of athleticism, strength, and courage. The professional rodeo circuit with its grueling schedule and six-figure purses remains a showcase for many of the same skills that built the American West.

BUCKING BRONC RIDERS, in neon and life, are emblems of the hard contests of the West.

COWBOYS ON THE CIRCUIT attend their event at a rodeo and then move on to the next show. Among the scenes represented: bronc riders waiting in the chutes; a bull rider holding for the buzzer signaling the end of the ride; a cowboy preparing to lasso a calf; and contestants readying their equipment.

247

YELLOWSTONE
NATIONAL PARK

Words like *beautiful* and *rugged* can't do justice to the towering forests and mountains, deep rivers and canyons, hot springs, and skyrocketing geysers found in Wyoming's Yellowstone National Park. The scenery in the granddaddy of our national parks has captivated attention ever since man first set foot in it, long before Yellowstone was designated a national landmark in 1872.

Prehistoric Indians used the area as a hunting ground. Fur trapper John Colter passed through for the first time in the early 1800s and brought back word of the magnitude and

ANGLING FOR TROUT (*left*) is more than a hobby for grizzlies, otters, osprey, and other animals native to the Yellowstone area. Fishing regulations are strictly enforced so that visitors can enjoy the sport without infringing on wildlife food supply.

potential riches of the area. Hunters, trappers, and, later, gold miners began to explore the region more purposefully. In 1871, an expedition of the U.S. Geological Survey charted the area for the first time. From that came a recognition of the superlative attributes of Yellowstone, and Congress was persuaded to set aside 2.2 million acres as the world's first national park.

OLD FAITHFUL GEYSER (*above*) sends its spray 130 feet into the air; there are more than 200 natural geysers in Yellowstone.

SMOKEY THE BEAR (*right*), a western folk hero, has been fighting forest fires for over forty years.

Old Faithful
INN

In the summer of 1904, a man-made wonder, the Old Faithful Inn, was added to Yellowstone National Park's natural phenomena. It was built to provide for well-to-do travelers accommodations more comfortable than those offered at the time by the spartan lodges in the area. Crafted by ax, adz, hammer, saw, and drawknife, the inn is a monumental example of rustic architecture set into the Wyoming wilderness. It was the work of a previously unknown and unheralded architect, twenty-nine-year-old Robert C. Reamer of Oberlin, Ohio.

FOREST OF WOOD-WORK (*left*) in the main lodge of Old Faithful Inn creates an imposing atrium space. Balcony rails and supports exhibit lodgepole pine's penchant for straight growth. The lacelike balusters reveal twisted forms, the result of insect infestation and disease.

Counting its two wing houses, the inn is 800 feet wide and 7 stories high. A 14-foot fireplace with 8 hearths and an 80-foot chimney stands in the lobby, a native stone obelisk of hand-quarried volcanic rock.

Even more surprising than the scale of the place is the fact that the entire building went up in the course of a single winter. The frame and roof were constructed first so workers could concentrate on the interior when cold weather

DORMERS SIT TEPEE-LIKE (*below*) on an immense shingle roof. The soaring design was meant to suggest the mountains that surround the Yellowstone country.

set in. Nevertheless, frostbite was a frequent problem for carpenters who toiled seven days a week in temperatures that dropped to 60 below. Local stone and timber was used, but additional materials had to be brought in by train, then hauled by horse for some 40 miles to the remote site. This included the complete central-heating system for the inn—steam-powered generator, boilers, pumps, radiators, and miles of pipes.

The timber palace with its cavernous central lobby still stands as a testament to the ingenuity of a young architect and the endurance and determination of a group

of frontier craftsmen who labored under difficult conditions to create the biggest log cabin in the West.

CRISSCROSSED LOGS (*below*) support the porte cochere and attest to a concern for detail on the part of the craftsmen who built the structure.

THE AMERICAN
Bison

When the United States Mint first coined the buffalo-head nickel, the American bison species was facing extinction. A systematic slaughter had reduced the great herds from 50,000,000 in the early 1800s to fewer than 1,000 by the turn of the century. Heroic conservation efforts reversed the tide, and the buffalo again thrives in protected wilderness reserves. The future of this spectacular animal, whose image is virtually synonymous with our American West, seems assured.

WILDERNESS SURVIVOR (*left and above*), **the American bison is a symbol of the endurance of the West.**

MONTANA SHED displays trophies of the wild and the road.

DIRECTORY OF STORES, GALLERIES, AND CRAFTSMEN

The following directory is listed alphabetically by state and shop name. Each store is then keyed according to specialty, with **A** for Antique or **C** for Contemporary

ARIZONA

Al Zuñi Indian Trading Co.
7090 Fifth Ave.
Scottsdale, AZ 85251
(602) 947-4977
● Indian jewelry and crafts.
C

Art America
9301 E. Shea Blvd.
Scottsdale, AZ 85260
(602) 661-8772
● Indian art, rugs, sand paintings, and pottery. Custom-made frames a specialty. **C**

Norma Clark Faux Finishes and Stencil Art
8701 E. Berridge Lane
Scottsdale, AZ 85250
(602) 991-8012
● Authentic Southwest Indian-design stencils. Brochure available for $3.00.
C

El Prado Galleries
Tlaquepaque Arts & Crafts Village
P.O. Box 1849
Sedona, AZ 86336
(602) 282-7390
● Fine contemporary and southwestern paintings and sculpture as well as new and unusual art forms. **C**

Gallery 10
7045 Third Ave.
Scottsdale, AZ 85251
(602) 994-0405
● Fine art objects of the Southwest. **C**

Hopi Arts and Crafts—Silvercraft Cooperative Guild
P.O. Box 37
Second Mesa, AZ 86043
(602) 734-2463
● Hopi overlay jewelry, Kachina dolls, coil and wicker plaques and baskets, Hopi pottery, textiles, and paintings. **C**

Elaine Horwitch Gallery
4211 N. Marshall Way
Scottsdale, AZ 85251
(602) 945-0791
● Contemporary American and Southwest paintings, graphics, sculpture, and mixed media. **C**

The Impeccable Pig
7042 East Indian School Rd.
Scottsdale, AZ 85251
(602) 941-1141
● Country furniture, quilts, and hooked rugs, and restaurant. **A, C**

Keams Canyon Arts & Crafts
P.O. Box 607, Hwy. #264
Keams Canyon, AZ 86034
(602) 738-2295
● Hopi Kachina dolls, Hopi pottery, and Navajo rugs. Wholesale and retail. **C**

Main Trail Store
7172 E. Main St.
Scottsdale, AZ 85251
(602) 990-7807
● Fine western Americana, contemporary and antique paintings, antique and contemporary bronzes, prehistoric pottery, antique baskets. **A, C**

National Native American Cooperative
P.O. Box 1000
San Carlos, AZ 85550
(602) 622-4900
● An American Indian cooperative representing 2,700 individual artists from over 100 tribes throughout the United States and Canada. A reference guide, the *Native American Directory*, is also available listing organizations, events, reserves, Indian stores, trading posts, and galleries. **C**

Navajo Silvercrafts
1713 West Buchanan
Phoenix, AZ 85007
(602) 253-1594
● Traditional Navajo-style jewelry. **C**

Sanders Galleries
6420 N. Campbell Ave.
Tucson, AZ 85718
(602) 299-1763
● Traditional western and contemporary southwestern

paintings, jewelry, baskets, pottery, and rugs. **C**

Sculptured Arts
P.O. Box 1849
Tlaquepaque Arts &
Crafts Village
Sedona, AZ 86336
(602) 282-4037
● One-of-a-kind and limited-edition sculptural art forms in bronze, terra-cotta, wood, steel, fiber, and ceramics. **C**

Paul S. Shepard/Primitive
Arts Limited
3026 E. Broadway
Tucson, AZ 85716
(602) 326-4852
● Fine historic and pre-historic American Indian items. **A**

Stone House Antiques
Paradise Valley, AZ 85006
(602) 952-1075
● By appointment only. Eighteenth- and early 19th-century American country furniture, quilts, weather vanes, samplers, and small collectibles. **A**

Thunderbird Lodge
Box 548, Canyon de Chelly
National Monument
Chinle, AZ 86503
(602) 674-5844
● Jeep tours into Canyon de Chelly. American Indian handmade arts and crafts in the heart of the Navajo reservation. **C**

Turquoise Buffalo
Kachina Building
252 North Hwy. #89A
Sedona, AZ 86336
(602) 282-5574
● Turquoise and silver jewelry. Old pawn items a specialty. **A, C**

The Wickenburg Gallery
67 N. Tegner
Wickenburg, AZ 85358
(602) 684-7047
● Western and wildlife original art by leading con-temporary artists; paintings, drawings, bronzes, wood sculpture, and engravings. **C**

CALIFORNIA
Marjorie Cahn Gallery
P.O. Box 2065
Los Gatos, CA 95031
(408) 356-0023
● Southwestern and native American art including paintings, graphics, textiles, bronzes, crafts, and artifacts as well as the Plains Indian Morning Star Quilt Collection of Florence Pulford. **C**

The Margaret Cavigga
Quilt Collection
8648 Melrose Ave.
Los Angeles, CA 90069
(310) 659-3020
● Antique quilts, coverlets, old hooked rugs, quilted toys, and dolls. **A, C**

East Meets West
658 N. Larchmont Blvd.
Hollywood, CA 90004
(213) 461-1389
● Antique quilts, tickings, vintage American flags, Indian blankets and pillows. **A**

Ophelia Johnson's Indian
Variety Shop
10256 Central Ave.
Montclair, CA 91763
(714) 625-2611
● Native American arts and crafts. Also a small museum on the premises with artifacts of the Indian war era. **C**

Richard Mulligan–Sunset
Cottage
8157 Sunset Blvd.
Los Angeles, CA 90046
(213) 650-8660
● Corn sconces and floor lamps, rugs, Santa Fe chairs, Southwest and Colonial tables, farm tools, slab tables. **A, C**

The Native American
Art Gallery
215 Windward Ave.
P.O. Box 1020
Venice, CA 90294
(310) 392-8465
● Prehistoric and antique arts of the American Indian,

specializing in the native arts of the Southwest. **A**

Red Desert
1640 Market St.
San Francisco, CA 94102
(415) 552-2800
● Cacti and other desert plants, also cactus wood, pottery. **C**

Reed Brothers
5000 Turner Rd.
Sebastopol, CA 95472
(707) 795-6261
● Reed Brothers designs and manufactures handmade, hand-carved furniture and garden accessories. The majority of the pieces are made of pine and redwood. Catalog available. **C**

Rosebud Gallery
57 Solano Ave.
Berkeley, CA 94707
(510) 525-6454
● Specializing in American Indian artifacts and American folk art. **A, C**

St. Helena Antiques
1231 Main St.
St. Helena, CA 94574
(707) 963-5878
● Early California antiques. **A**

The Snow Goose
1010 Torrey Pines Rd.
La Jolla, CA 92037
(619) 454-4893
● American and southwest-ern furniture and folk art, interior design. **A, C**

Trails West Gallery
1476 South Coast Hwy.
Laguna Beach, CA 92651
(714) 494-7888

Trails West Gallery
26822 Ortega Hwy.
San Juan Capistrano, CA
92675
(714) 496-0100
● Fine western bronzes and
oil paintings by well-known
artists, Navajo rugs, Indian
pottery, jewelry, Kachina
dolls, saddles, spurs, branding irons. **A, C**

Vanderbilt and Company
1429 Main St.
St. Helena, CA 94574
(707) 963-1010
● Imported and domestic
furnishings for the house
and garden. **C**

Wild Goose Chase
S. Coast Plaza Village
1631 Sunflower Ave.
Santa Ana, CA 92704
(714) 966-2722
● Vintage Beacon blankets,
painted furniture, and art
pottery. **A**

Wounded Knee Indian
Art Gallery
2413 Wilshire Blvd.
Santa Monica, CA 90403
(310) 394-0159
● Pueblo pottery, Navajo
rugs, Hopi Kachina dolls,
original paintings and graph-

ics, beadwork, fine jewelry,
masks, fetishes, sand paintings, sculpture, and baskets.
A, C

Yat-Ta-Hey Indian
Trading Post
P.O. Box 2732
6495 Washington St.
Napa Valley, Yountville, CA
94599
(707) 944-8012
● Contemporary Indian arts
and crafts. **C**

COLORADO
Path of the Sun Images
3020 Lowell Blvd.
Denver, CO 80211
(303) 477-8442
● Gallery, cultural consul-
tants, beadwork repair. **C**

Sacks Fifth Ave. Antiques
222 Fifth Ave.
P.O. Drawer 1878
Ouray, CO 81427
(303) 325-4278
● Glass, china, linens, primi-
tives, collectibles. Open
May 1–October 15. **A**

Shepler Gallery
103 Bear Creek Ave.
P.O. Box 374
Morrison, CO 80465
(303) 697-5311
● Authentic Indian artifacts
from the Plains and
Southwest Indians, Hopi
baskets and Kachina dolls;
Navajo rugs and sand paintings, Pueblo pottery and
paintings. **C**

Jane Smith
The Brand Building
201 S. Galena
Aspen, CO 81611
(303) 925-6105
● Western furniture by L. D.
Burke III, Stallion boots,
leather goods and accessories.
C

Mark Winter Company
1 Old Durango Rd.
P.O. Box 1570
Pagosa Springs, CO 81147
(303) 264-5957
● Old Navajo rugs and blankets, Saltillo serapes, Pueblo
and Rio Grande blankets. **A**

DISTRICT OF COLUMBIA
Counts Western Store
4905 Wisconsin Ave. N.W.
Washington, D.C. 20016
(202) 362-1757
● Western clothing and
boots for men, women, and
children. **C**

The Indian Craft Shop
1849 C St.
Department of Interior
Washington, D.C. 20240
(202) 737-4381
(202) 208-4056
● Pottery, jewelry, basketry,
sand paintings, and a large
collection of Hopi Kachinas
handmade by native
Americans. **C**

Marston Luce
1314 21st St. N.W.
Washington, D.C. 20036
(202) 775-9460
● Pre-1880s furniture, mirrors, architectural objects,
paintings, weather vanes, and
quilts. **A**

FLORIDA
One Hand Clapping
432 Española Way
Miami Beach, FL 33319
(305) 532-0507
● Specializing in vintage
fabrics. **A**

GEORGIA

Flynn-Devereux
3927 Oberlin Court
Tucker, Georgia 30084
(404) 491-0929
● Furniture, lighting and
accessories made from naturally shed antlers. **C**

IDAHO

Blue Haven Antiques
102 Blue Haven Lane
Ketchum, ID 83340
(208) 726-1176
● Glass, china, furniture,
and primitives. **C**

L&C Western Trading Post
Rt. 2, Box 105B
Kamiah, ID 83536
(208) 935-2601
● A large collection of western and Indian material and
genuine artifacts for sale. **A**

Marsh's Trading Post
1105 36th St. N.
Lewiston, ID 83501
(208) 743-5778
● Antiques, western and
Indian artifacts. **A, C**

Anne Reed Gallery
620 Sun Valley Rd.
Ketchum, ID 83340
(208) 726-3036
● Contemporary quilts,
rustic log and peeled willow
furniture. **C**

ILLINOIS

Mark and Lisa McCormick
8837 Schmaltz Rd.
St. Jacob, IL 62281
(618) 667-7789
● Regional country painted
furniture, textiles, folk
art, and Americana. By
appointment only. **A**

INDIANA

Michael Boone Coppersmith
11044 N. Carthage Pike
Carthage, IN 46115
(317) 565-6521
● Featuring Michael Boone's
restored coppersmith's shop
and copperwares. **A, C**

LOUISIANA

Bep's Antiques
2051 Magazine St.
New Orleans, LA 70130
(504) 525-7726
● Eighteenth- and 19th-
century furniture, tools, phar-
maceutical and medical
objects, specializing in old
apothecary bottles. **A**

Gallery of the Mesas
2010 Rapides Ave.
Alexandria, LA 71301
(318) 442-6372
● Featuring the work of
Charles H. Jeffress; silkscreen,
inkless intaglio, and collages.
C

MAINE

Paula Anderson's Baskets
Box 136
North New Portland, ME
04961
(207) 628-3221

● Traditional Shaker as well
as Indian-inspired large and
small woven containers. **C**

Kawi Designs
P.O. Box 453
Old Town, ME 04468
(207) 827-3447
● Indian jewelry, beadwork,
and quillwork. **C**

Marston House
Main St. at Middle
Wiscasset, ME 04578
(207) 882-6010
● Bed & Breakfast and
Country Store specializing in
antique 1840s New England
painted furniture and vintage
homespun fabrics. **A**

MASSACHUSETTS

Courtney's
754 Main St.
Osterville, MA 02655
(508) 428-1022
● Custom-designed gold and
turquoise jewelry, baskets,
New Mexican pottery, soap-
stone carvings, Southwest
weaving, and sand paintings.
A, C

T. P. Saddleblanket &
Trading Co.
304 Main St.
Great Barrington, MA 01230
(413) 528-6500
● Wild West clothing,
furniture, vintage blankets
and birdhouses. **A, C**

MINNESOTA

The Wooden Bird
11001 Hampshire South
Bloomington, MN 55438
(800) 328-3615
● Publisher of wildlife
and western limited-edition
lithographs with retail
galleries in Minnesota,
Illinois, California, Texas,
Arizona, and Wyoming. **C**

Woodland Indian Crafts
Minneapolis American
Indian Center
1530 E. Franklin Ave.
Minneapolis, MN 55404
(612) 874-7766
● All Indian handcrafts,
beads, supplies, records,
tapes, and jewelry. **C**

MISSOURI

Jack Parker Antiques
4652 Shaw at Kings Hwy.
St. Louis, MO 63110
(314) 773-3320
● Cultural artifacts of the
American Indian (pottery,
baskets, textiles, beadwork,
etc.) plus paintings by
Midwest and Southwest
artists. **A**

Spirit of America
1919 Park Ave.
St. Louis, MO 63104
(314) 241-9992
● Specializing in fine
American quilts circa
1850–1940. Crystalline pottery from Arizona, antique
linens, hooked rugs, some
handmade wearable art. By
appointment only. **A, C**

MONTANA

Doug Allards
Highway 93
St. Ignatius, MT 59865
(406) 745-2951
● Antique American
Indian art. **A**

Cuts the Rope Gallery
Box 1024
Hays, MT 59527
(406) 673-3612
● Western art by Clarence
Cuts the Rope in oil, water-
color, pastel, ink; sculpture.
Specializing in wildlife and
portraits of the traditional and
contemporary Indian of the
Northern Plains. **C**

NEBRASKA

Anderson/O'Brien Gallery
8724 Pacific St.
Countryside Village
Omaha, NB 68114
(402) 390-0717
● Rare antique prints and
original art from the Plains
and Plateau area including
19th-century American
Indian beadwork, baskets,
and related artifacts. **A**

NEVADA

Sierra Galleries
P.O. Box 5800
Stateline, NV 89449
(702) 588-8500
● Dealers in new and old art
of the American West. **A, C**

NEW HAMPSHIRE

Burt Savage Lodge
Rt. 126, Box 11
Center Stratford, NH 03815
(603) 269-7411
● Rustic furniture and acces-
sories. By appointment only.
A, C

NEW MEXICO

Adobe Gallery
413 Romero N.W.
Albuquerque, NM 87104
(505) 243-8485
● Authentic Southwest
Indian arts and crafts, partic-
ularly of the New Mexico and
Arizona Pueblo Indians. **C**

Back at the Ranch
235 Don Gaspar St.
Santa Fe, NM 87501
(505) 989-8110
● Vintage clothing shop specializing in clothing made
from Beacon and Pendleton
blankets. A line of custom-
made boots as well. **A, C**

Blue Rose
131 W. San Francisco St.
Santa Fe, NM 87501
(505) 983-8807
● Soft leather clothing of
original design (skirts, prairie
shirts, etc.) **C**

Centinela Traditional Arts
HCR 64, Box 4
Centinela Ranch
Chimayo, NM 85722
(505) 351-2180
● Traditional New Mexico
Spanish Colonial weaving. **C**

Cristofs
106 W. San Francisco St.
Santa Fe, NM 87501
(505) 988-9881
● Specializing in exceptional
quality contemporary Navajo
rugs, wall hangings, and
handcrafted jewelry, as well
as other native American
art. **C**

Desert Son
725 Canyon Rd.
Santa Fe, NM 87501
(505) 982-9499
● Fine western boots and
hats, handmade belts, moc
casins, old pawn silver, but-
tons, beadwork, and bags.
A, C

Dewey Galleries, Ltd.
74 E. San Francisco St.
Santa Fe, NM 87501
(505) 982-8478
● Fine, rare native American
and Hispanic American folk
art, furniture, jewelry, pottery,
textiles, and paintings. **A**

El Prado Galleries
Plaza Mercado
Santa Fe, NM 87501
(505) 988-2906
● Southwestern, contempo-
rary, and Impressionist paintings and sculpture. **C**

Felix Indian Jewelry
1001 W. 66th Ave.
P.O. Box 195
Gallup, NM 87301
(505) 722-5369
● Authentic (primarily
Navajo) Indian jewelry made
on the premises. Catalog
available. **C**

First American Traders of
Gallup Inc.
2201 W. 66th Ave.
Gallup, NM 87301
(505) 722-6601
● Fine, authentic American
Indian handmade jewelry.
American Indian arts and
crafts. **C**

Galeria de Alamo
Tenth & New York Ave.
Alamogordo, NM 88310
(505) 437-8740
● Fine western paintings by
contemporary artists. **C**

Austin "Slim" Green
Rt. 4, P.O. Box 88
Tesuque, NM 87574
(505) 982-2092
● Custom work only. **C**

Elaine Horwitch Gallery
129 W. Palace Ave.
Santa Fe, NM 87501
(505) 988-8997
● Contemporary American
and Southwest paintings,
graphics, sculpture, and
mixed media art. **C**

Indian Trader—West
204 W. San Francisco St.
Santa Fe, NM 87501
(505) 988-5776
● Fine Indian crafts and
collector's items. **A, C**

Institute of American Indian
Arts Museum Shop
108 Cathedral Place
Santa Fe, NM 87501
(505) 988-6281
● A nonprofit sales outlet for
arts and crafts produced by
students and alumni of the
National Native American
College. Items include paintings, sculpture, beadwork,
quillwork, textiles, weaving,
baskets, jewelry, and Indian
"traditional techniques" such
as costumes. **C**

Jackalope Pottery
2820 Cerrillos Rd.
Santa Fe, NM 87501
(505) 471-8539
● Primitives from Mexico
(oxen yokes, carts, pots, etc.).
Also antique and reproduction Colonial furniture. **A, C**

Kania-Ferrin Gallery
662 Canyon Rd.
Santa Fe, NM 87501
(505) 982-8767
● Antique American Indian
art (concentrating on Indian
basketry) and southwestern
memorabilia. **A**

La Bodega
667 Canyon Rd.
Santa Fe, NM 87501
(505) 982-8043
● Artifacts and decorator
items of early western
America. **A, C**

Madrid Earthenware Pottery
Box 300, Main St.
Madrid, NM 87033
(505) 471-3450
● Featuring red earthenware
pottery by Joni Conrad,
decorated with blue-and-
white animal designs, and
the work of other fine New
Mexican potters. **C**

Morning Star Gallery
513 Canyon Rd.
Santa Fe, NM 87501
(505) 982-8187
● Pre-1900 American Indian
art, specializing in the Plains
Buffalo culture. **A**

Nedra Matteucci's Fenn
Galleries
1075 Paseo de Peralta
Santa Fe, NM 87501
(505) 982-4631
● Specializing in paintings
by the old Taos and Santa Fe
artists, the Brandywine,
Hudson River, and Ashcan

schools, and masters of the
American West. American
bronze and stone sculpture.
Old pottery, baskets, bead-
work, and jewelry of the
American Indian. **C**

Robert F. Nichols Gallery
419 Canyon Rd.
Santa Fe, NM 87501
(505) 982-2145
● American folk art and
Indian art, specializing in
Indian pottery of the
American Southwest. **A**

Oke Oweenge Crafts
Cooperative
P.O. Box 1095
San Juan Pueblo, NM 87566
(505) 852-2372
● Traditional Pueblo arts and
crafts, specializing in San Juan
Pueblo embroidery, red pot-
tery, beading, and weaving. **C**

Ortega's Weaving Shop
P.O. Box 325
Jct. S.R. 76 at S.R. 520
Chimayo, NM 87522
(505) 351-4215
● Quality Rio Grande weav-
ing by a family whose Spanish
ancestors brought the craft to
New Mexico in the 1600s. **C**

The Gerald Peters Gallery
439 Camino del Monte Sol
Santa Fe, NM 87501
(505) 988-8961
● Classic western
American painting and art
of the Taos school. **C**

Prairie Edge
102 E. Water St.
Santa Fe, NM 87501
(505) 984-1336
● Plains Indian art,
artifacts, and jewelry. **C**

The Rainbow Man
107 E. Palace Ave.
Santa Fe, NM 87501
(505) 982-8706
● Specializing in Indian trade
blankets and Indian jewelry.
A

James Reid, Ltd.
114 E. Palace Ave.
Santa Fe, NM 87501
(505) 988-1147
out-of-state: (800) 545-2056
● The gallery features antique
and contemporary arts of the
Southwest. The workshop
employs twelve silversmiths
who create original designs in
silver and gold. Also, specializing in antique Indian art.
A, C

Millicent Rogers
Museum Store
1504 Museum Rd.
P.O. Box A
Taos, NM 87571
(505) 758-4316
● Native American and
Spanish arts and crafts. **C**

Santa Fe House of Books
Box 23503
Santa Fe, NM 87502
(505) 473-5161
● Rare, out-of-print, and
contemporary books on the
Southwest, the West, and

Native American Indians. By appointment only. **A, C**

Simply Santa Fe
72 E. San Francisco St.
Santa Fe, NM 87501
(505) 988-3100
● Clothing, jewelry, home furnishings, and lamps. **A**

Jane Smith
125 W. San Francisco St.
Santa Fe, NM 87501
● Western jewelry, clothing, and home furnishings. **C**

Square Deal Shoe Shop
304 Johnson St.
Santa Fe, NM 87501
(505) 982-6469
● Handmade boots and shoes for men and women using the best materials and workmanship, and guaranteed to fit. **C**

Taos Furniture
232 Galisteo St.
P.O. Box 5555
Santa Fe, NM 87502
(505) 988-1229
● Traditional and contemporary New Mexican furnishings. Makers of Taos furniture. **C**

Tiqua Gallery
812 Canyon Rd.
Santa Fe, NM 87501
(505) 984-8704
● Antique Indian art and Spanish Colonial art. **A**

Trailblazer
210 West Hill
Gallup, NM 87301
(505) 722-5051
● Indian jewelry, sand paintings, Kachinas, leather, rugs and pottery. **C**

Trujillo's Weaving Shop
Box 18-A
Chimayo, NM 87522
(505) 351-4457
● Specializing in hand-loomed rugs and blankets in different sizes, stripes, and geometric designs. **C**

Tobe Turpen's Indian Trading Co.
1710 South 2nd St.
Gallup, NM 87301
(505) 722-3806
● In the Indian trading business since 1929. Wholesale and retail Indian jewelry, rugs, pottery, baskets, Kachinas, sand paintings, oil and watercolor paintings, carvings. **A, C**

White Feather Trading Co.
326 San Felipe N.W.
Albuquerque, NM 87104
Mailing address:
P.O. Box 7415
Albuquerque, NM 87194
(505) 243-5115
● Plains Indians arts and crafts. Beadwork, hides, pelts, feathers. **C**

NEW YORK

ABC Carpet & Home
888 Broadway
New York, NY 10003
(212) 473-3000
● Reproduction and antique rustic furniture, decorative objects, and rugs. **A, C**

Adirondack Store & Gallery
109 Saranac Ave.
Lake Placid, NY 12946
(518) 523-2646
● Prints, books, trophies, antlers, and reproduction and antique furniture. **A, C**

American Indian Crafts
719 Broad St.
Salamanca, NY 14779
(716) 945-1225
● Indian owned and operated. Unique Indian handmade products from New York's Seneca tribe and many other tribes. **C**

Ruby Beets
Poxabogue Rd. & Route 27
Bridgehampton, NY 11937
Mailing address:
Box 596
Wainscott, NY 11975
(516) 537-2802
● Specializing in country painted furniture. **A**

Bird in Hand Antiques
Main St.
Bridgehampton, NY 11932
(516) 537-3838
● Eighteenth- and 19th-century American furniture, folk art and decorative accessories. **A**

Laura Fisher Antiques
1050 Second Ave.
Gallery 84
New York, NY 10021
(212) 838-2596
● Antique quilts, Beacon blankets, and mirrors. **A**

Hope & Wilder Home
454 Broome St.
New York, NY 10013
(212) 966-9010
● Antique textiles, painted furniture, iron bedframes as well as the Hope & Wilder Collection of furniture and fabrics by the yard. **A, C**

Mark Humphrey Gallery
95 Main St.
Southampton, NY 11968
(516) 283-3113
● Original, signed graphics of American Indian themes. Baskets. Posters by Southwest artists. **C**

Kelter-Malce
74 Jane St.
New York, NY 10014
(212) 989-6760
● Pendleton blankets; birch bark frames; Old hickory, Molesworth, and twig furni-

ture; textiles; beadwork; specializing in historic American Indian pottery. By appointment only. **A, C**

Robert Kinnaman at Ramaekers, Inc.
Main St.
Bridgehampton, NY 11932
(516) 537-3838
● Eighteenth- and 19th-century furniture and decorative objects. Folk art. **A**

Billy Martin's Western Wear Inc.
812 Madison Ave.
New York, NY 10021
(212) 861-3100
● Handmade and custom-made leather apparel. Furs, belts, silver, and antique buckles and jewelry plus a line of quality handmade boots for men and women. **A, C**

Susan P. Meisel Decorative Arts Gallery
141 Prince St.
New York, NY 10012
(212) 254-0137
● Americana and folk art artifacts. **A, C**

Susan Parrish Antiques
390 Bleecker St.
New York, NY 10014
(212) 645-5020
● Quilts, Beacon and Pendleton blankets, American Indian jewelry, late 19th- and early 20th-century Navajo weavings and rare Navajo flatware. **A**

Morgan Rank Gallery
4 Newtown Lane
East Hampton, NY 11937
(516) 324-7615
● American primitive art, sculpture, and paintings. **A**

Paula Rubenstein, Ltd.
65 Prince St.
New York, NY 10012
(212) 966-8954
● Old Beacon and Pendleton blankets, hooked rugs, ticking, textiles, tramp art, and rustic furniture. **A**

Trotta-Bono American Indian Art
P.O. Box 34
Shrub Oak, NY 10588
(914) 528-6604
● Specializing in American Indian art. By appointment only. **C**

Barbara Trujillo Antiques
Main St.
Bridgehampton, NY 11932
(516) 537-3838
● Specializing in antique Indian jewelry. **A**

Turtle Gift Shop
25 Rainbow Mall
Niagara Falls, NY 14303
(716) 284-2427
● American Indian handcrafts and art. Silver and turquoise jewelry, beadwork, leatherwork, quilts, cornhusk dolls,

sculpture, bone jewelry, porcupine quillwork, baskets, sweet-grass crafts, and an assortment of unique items such as cradles, pipes, vests, headdresses, and belts. **C**

Wolfman•Gold & Good Company
116 Greene St.
New York, NY 10012
● Vintage cast-iron beds, painted furniture, and rustic birdhouses. **A, C**

Zona
97 Greene St.
New York, NY 10012
(212) 925-6750
● New Mexican Mission furniture; ponderosa pine, contemporary, and authentic reproduction furniture; southwestern native plant materials; Navajo rugs. **C**

NORTH CAROLINA
Qualla Arts and Crafts Mutual, Inc.
Box 310
Cherokee, NC 28719
(704) 497-3103
● An Indian-owned and operated crafts cooperative featuring both traditional and contemporary merchandise. **C**

Tuscorora Indian Handcraft Shop
Rt. 4, Box 172
Maxton, NC 28364
(919) 844-3352
● All handmade leatherwork, beadwork, and silver. **C**

Wayahsti Indian Arts and Traditions
P.O. Box 130
Hollister, NC 27844
(919) 586-4519

● Stone sculpture, beadwork, buckskin bags, clothing, stone bowls, ceremonial pipes, powwow drums; specializing in handmade flutes. Indian owned and operated. **C**

OKLAHOMA
Colonial Antiques
1329 E. 15th St.
Tulsa, OK 74120
(918) 585-3865
● American Indian textiles and baskets. **A**

The Galleria
1630 W. Lindsey
Norman, OK 73069
(405) 329-1225
● Specializing in native American and western art: painting, sculpture, pottery, jewelry, weaving, and basketry by leading American artists. **C**

Bill Glass Jr. Studio
HCR 64, Box 1410
Locust Grove, OK 74352
(918) 479-8884
● Original ceramic stoneware
sculpture and pottery by a
Cherokee artist. By appoint-
ment only. **C**

Mister Indian's Cowboy Store
1000 S. Main St.
Sapulpa, OK 74066
(918) 224-6511
● Custom-made, special,
Indian contemporary and
traditional design. **C**

Monkapeme
205 N.E. Seventh
P.O. Box 457
Perkins, OK 74066
(405) 547-6511
● Custom-made, special,
Indian contemporary and tra-
ditional designs. **C**

Snake Creek Workshop
P.O. Box 147
Rose, OK 74364
(918) 479-8867
● Necklaces, earrings,
bracelets, hatbands, belts, and
other jewelry by Knokovtee
Scott, a designer reviving an
art form from the temple
mound period of the Creek
and Cherokee tribes. **C**

OREGON
Stars and Splendid Company
Antique Malls
7027 S. E. Milwaukie Ave.
Portland, OR 97292
(503) 239-0346

● Painted country furniture,
textiles, quilts, collectibles,
jewelry, vintage clothing and
sport equipment. **A**

PENNSYLVANIA
Crown and Eagle
Antiques, Inc.
P.O. Box 181
New Hope, PA 18938
(215) 794-7972
● American Indian art and
artifacts. Old pawn and fine-
quality new jewelry. Rugs,
basketry, beadwork, weapons,
and pottery. **C, A**

East Meets West
209 Market St.
Lewisburg, PA 17837
(717) 523-3945
● Antique quilts, Indian
blankets and pillows, vintage
American flags. **A**

Theo B. Price Country Store
Rt. 191
Cresco, PA 18326
(717) 595-2501
● Country store. Folk art. **C**

RHODE ISLAND
Stephen Mack
Chase Hill Farm
Ashaway, RI 02804
(401) 377-8041
● Builder of houses using
disassembled period antique
structures combined with
new design. **A, C**

TEXAS
Apple Tree Antiques
Old Ingram Loop
Ingram, TX 78025
(210) 367-4200
● American country pieces.
Old branding irons, saddles,
sun-bleached steer heads. **A**

Country Cottage Antiques
247 E. Main
Fredericksburg, TX 78624
(210) 997-8549
● Specializing in southwestern, English, and French
country as well as primitive
furniture. **A**

The Country Gentlemen
221 E. 11th St.
Houston, TX 77007
(713) 880-9165
● Mennonite and Mexican
Colonial furniture and
accessories. Tarahumara
Indian pottery. American
country furniture, folk art
and accessories. **A**

Country Things, Etc.
414 East Main St.
Fredericksburg, TX 78624
(210) 997-2910
● A wide assortment of
country accessories. **C**

The Gypsy Savage
1509 Indiana Ave.
Houston, TX 77006
(713) 528-0897
● Laces and linens, Victorian
and Edwardian dresser accessories. **A**

Horsefeathers
215 Old Ingram Loop
Ingram, TX 78025
(210) 367-5020
● Antiques, paintings, hand-loomed rugs, and Mexican folk art. **A**

Jabberwocky
207 East Main St.
Fredericksburg, TX 78624
(210) 997-7071
● Old and new textiles, vintage clothing, and replicas of vintage designs. **A, C**

Naranjo of Santa Fe in the Village
2418 Rice Blvd.
Houston, TX 77005
(713) 660-9690
● Pottery, weaving, carvings, painting, graphics, artifacts, custom-designed jewelry. **A, C**

Room Service
4354 Lovers' Lane
Dallas, TX 75225
(214) 369-7666
● Complete line of home furnishings with over 500 fabrics in stock. **A, C**

The Royers' Round Top Cafe
"On the Square"
Round Top, TX 78954
(409) 249-3611
(800) 86-ROYERS
(800) 624-PIES
● Western eight-table cafe open on the weekends featuring homemade pies. Specialties of the house are the pepper sauce and five different vinegars packed in heart-shaped, refillable bottles.

The Settler's Antiques
725 North Main St.
Boerne, TX 78006
(210) 249-8919
● Hill Country antiques mixed with New England shipments. **A**

Southwest Images Gallery
123 E. Main St.
Fredericksburg, TX 78624
(210) 997-8688
● Featuring southwestern fine arts and crafts, paintings, bronze, and unique gifts. **A**

Stelzig's
3123 S. Post Oak
Houston, TX 77056
(713) 629-7779

● Everything for the western and English horse and rider. Gift items, holsters, custom belts, leatherwork, and repairs. **C**

Texas Traditions
2222 College Ave.
Austin, TX 78704
(512) 443-4447
● Custom-made and -designed boots. Domestic and exotic leathers. By appointment only. **C**

Voigt House Antiques
308 E. San Antonio St.
New Braunfels, TX 78130
(512) 625-7072
● Country primitives; cut glass; American and European pine, oak, and walnut; coins and gifts. **A**

VERMONT
T.P. Saddleblanket
& Trading Co.
Manchester Center
Rt. 11 & 30
Manchester, VT 05255
(802) 362-9888
● Wild West clothing, vintage

furniture, blankets, and birdhouses. **A, C**

WASHINGTON
Akers Taxidermist
1303 Astor St.
Bellingham, WA 98225
(206) 734-1085
● Indian-type drums, leather paintings, black bear rugs, and other fur rugs. **C**

Ruby Montana's
Pinto Pony Ltd.
603 Second Ave.
Seattle, WA 98104
(206) 621-PONY
● Variety store specializing in vintage furnishings and decorative objects and western collectibles. **A, C**

Sacred Circle Gallery
of American Indian Art
3801 Government Way
Seattle, WA 98121
(206) 285-4425
● Featuring fine traditional and contemporary American Indian artists. **C**

Suquamish Museum Store
P.O. Box 498
Sandy Hook Rd.
Suquamish, WA 98392
(206) 598-3311
● Specializing in traditional
Coast Salish arts and crafts,
both replicas and works by
living artists and craftsmen.
C

WYOMING
Big Horn Taxidermy
5060 Coffeen
Sheridan, WY 82801
(307) 672-2813
● Custom taxidermy work. C

The Boardwalk, Inc.
1951 Snowy Range Rd.
Laramie, WY 82070
(307) 742-3977
● A large selection of Indian
crafts and custom-made harness and saddlery. **A, C**

Fort Washakie Trading Co.
and R.V. Greeves Art Gallery
Wind River Indian
Reservation
P.O. Box 428
Fort Washakie, WY 82514
(307) 332-3557
● American Indian arts and
crafts. Antique Indian collec-
tor's pieces. **A, C**

Jackson Hole Furniture
235 Crabtree Lane
Jackson, WY 83001
(307) 733-7503
● Custom shop specializing
in rawhide chairs made from
cowhide. C

King's Saddlery
184 N. Main
Sheridan, WY 82801
(307) 672-2702
● Manufacturers of lariats
and saddlery goods. C

Lodgepole Furniture Mfg.
S.R. Box 15
Jackson, WY 83001
(307) 733-3199
● Pole and rawhide furniture
made with lodgepole pine
(trees so named because the
Indians used them to build
their lodges and tepees). C

Longhorn Saddle Shop
1878 Snowy Range Rd.
Laramie, WY 82070
(307) 745-8449
● Saddles and all other horse
tack made by hand. Special
service: restoring old saddles
and gear. C

Sam Senkow
Castle Kirkstein
Bondurant, WY 82922
● Western antiques, hand-
crafted Fur Trade-era items
from weapons to clothing,
all by western craftsmen.
Write for appointment. **A**

Sweet Water Ranch
531 16th St.
P.O. 398
Cody, WY 82414
(307) 527-4044
● Specializing in a line of
reproduction Molesworth furniture as well as custom
work. C

CHRIS MEAD

DIRECTORY OF MUSEUMS AND HISTORIC SITES

ALABAMA
Birmingham Museum of Art
2000 8th Ave. North
Birmingham, AL 35203
(205) 254-2566
● Art of the Old West.
Bronze sculptures, paintings,
drawings, and lithographs.
American Indian art and artifacts from the Northwest
Coast, Plains, Southwest, and
Alabama Mound culture
tribes, including clothing and
accessories, basketry, pottery,
headdresses, masks, and
blankets.

ARIZONA
Casa Grande Ruins National
Monument and Visitors'
Center
P.O. Box 518
Coolidge, AZ 85228
(602) 723-3172
● The monument grounds
contain about sixty prehistoric sites, preserving a
small sample of the remains
of a once widespread civilization, the prehistoric-Indian
farmers of the Gila Valley,
the Hohokam.

Colorado River Indian
Tribes Museum
Rt. 1, Box 23-B
Parker, AZ 85344
(602) 669-9211
● A collection dealing with
the prehistory and history of

the four tribes of the reservation: Mojave, Chemehuevi,
Navajo, and Hopi.

Desert Caballeros
Western Museum
P.O. Box 1446
21 N. Frontier St.
Wickenburg, AZ 85358
(602) 684-2272
● The museum covers
14,000 square feet and is
divided into several areas,
including a Hall of History,
Period Rooms, Street Scenes,
a Mineral Room, and an
Indian Room dealing with the
Wickenburg area, as well as a
Western Art Gallery contain-
ing numerous bronzes and
paintings by past and present
western masters.

Grand Canyon National Park
Study Collection
P.O. Box 129
Grand Canyon, AZ 86023
(602) 638-7769
● A collection of material
on the Grand Canyon,
including prehistoric and historic artifacts, natural history
specimens, documents,
photographs, and art.

Mohave Museum of History
and Arts
400 West Beale St.
Kingman, AZ 86401
(602) 753-3195
● A collection of Indian basketry, pottery, and beadwork
from the Hualapai and
Mojave tribes.

Museum of Northern Arizona
Rt. 4, Box 720
Flagstaff, AZ 86001
(602) 774-5211
● Collections dealing with
archaeology, ethnology, geolo-
gy, paleontology, zoology,
botany, and Indian and
Southwest arts and crafts.
The gift shop carries contemporary southwestern native
American arts and crafts and
the book shop specializes in
books and posters of the
Southwest.

Navajo National Monument
Visitor Center
Navajo National Monument
HC 71, Box 35
Tonalea, AZ 86044
(602) 672-2366
● Guided hikes during the
summer months to the Indian
cliff dwellings ruins. The visitors' center has a museum
with exhibits on the prehistoric Anasazi Indians and a
smaller exhibit dealing with
contemporary Navajo Indians
of the area.

Pueblo Grande Museum
4619 E. Washington St.
Phoenix, AZ 85034
(602) 495-0901
● The museum consists of a
prehistoric Hohokam ruin,
a permanent exhibit area
explaining the Hohokam,
and a changing gallery
featuring various southwestern Indian groups.

CALIFORNIA
Cabot's Old Indian
Pueblo Museum
67616 E. Desert View Ave.
Desert Hot Springs, CA
92240
(619) 329-7610
● Using only his hands, the
earth, and cast-off materials,
Cabot Yerxa erected this thir-
ty-five-room Hopi structure
over a period of twenty years.

California State
Indian Museum
2618 K St.
Sacramento, CA 95816
(916) 324-0971
● One of the largest collections of California Indian
baskets in the state.

Clarke Memorial
Museum, Inc.
240 E St.
Eureka, CA 95501
(707) 443-1947
● A collection of over 1,500
baskets from the Yurok,
Karok, and Hupa tribes of
northwestern California as
well as dance regalia and
stonework from northwestern
California.

Julian Pioneer Museum
2811 Washington St.
P.O. Box 511
Julian, CA 92036
(619) 765-0227
● Local Indian baskets,
ollas, and artifacts.

Lake County Museum
255 N. Main St.
Lakeport, CA 95453
Mailing address:
255 N. Forbes St.
Lakeport, CA 95453
(707) 263-4555
● Collections and exhibits
on the Pomo Indian tribe,
including an outstanding
basket collection.

Maturango Museum of
Indian Wells Valley
100 East Las Flores
Ridgecrest, CA 93556
Mailing address:
Box 1776
Ridgecrest, CA 93556
(619) 375-6900

● Local Indian artifacts and
displays, some mining artifacts.

Natural History Museum of
Los Angeles County
900 Exposition Blvd.
Los Angeles, CA 90007
(213) 744-3466
● Collection of ethnological
and archaeological artifacts of
western North American
Indians.

Pio Pico Museum
6003 Pioneer Blvd.
Whittier, CA 90606
(310) 695-1217
● Thirteen-room 1852 adobe
building with furnishings
from the 1850s to 1870s.

San Diego Museum of Man
1350 El Prado
Balboa Park
San Diego, CA 92101
Mailing address:
P.O. Box 41558
Los Angeles, CA 90041-0558
(619) 239-2001
● Southwestern Indian
archaeology and ethnology,
physical anthropology, pho-
tographs, and a library.

Southwest Museum
234 Museum Drive
Los Angeles, CA 90065
(213) 221-2163
● Prehistoric, historic, and
contemporary American
Indian art and artifacts. The
facilities include a research
library and a museum store as
well as the Casa de Adobe, a
re-creation of an 1850s-era
Spanish California hacienda
located at 4605 North
Figueroa, three blocks from
the museum proper. The Casa
features rooms with period
furnishings and a gallery with
rotating exhibits.

Will Rogers State
Historic Park
14253 Sunset Blvd.
Pacific Palisades, CA 90272
(310) 454-8212
● Will Rogers's ranch home
is open for tours daily. The
ranch home collection
includes paintings and sculptures by Charles M. Russell
as well as several examples
of Indian artwork, primarily
Navajo rugs.

ProRodeo Hall of Fame
& Museum of the American
Cowboy
101 ProRodeo Drive
Colorado Springs, CO 80919
(719) 593-8840
● The hall features two multi-
media theaters presenting the
history and story of cowboys
and rodeo. The museum collection is composed of cowboy artifacts and rodeo cham-
pions' artifacts. There is also
an art gallery with changing
exhibits.

CONNECTICUT

Tantaquidgeon Indian
Museum
1819 Norwich-New London
Tpk.
Uncasville, CT 06382
(203) 848-9145
● The purpose of the museum is to preserve and perpetuate the history and traditions
of the Mohegan and other
Indian tribes. Displays in
the Northern Plains section
include work in parfleche,
porcupine quillwork, and
beadwork. The southwestern
and California sections
contain pottery, rugs, and
baskets.

INDIANA

Eiteljorg Museum of
American Indian and
Western Art
500 W. Washington
Indianapolis, IN 46204
(317) 636-9378
● Collection of paintings,
drawings, and bronzes relat-

COLORADO

Baca & Bloom Houses
Pioneer Museum
300 E. Main St.
P.O. Box 472
Trinidad, CO 81082
(719) 846-7217
● This Colorado Historical
Society regional museum
complex, located on the Santa
Fe Trail, features the adobe,
two-story, territorial style Baca
House. The nine-room house
is restored and displays
Spanish-Colonial objects.
The outlying adobe buildings
house the Pioneer Museum
and exhibits of western
expansion. The Bloom House,
an 1880s Second Empire
Mansion, is restored and displays Victorian objects in a
southwestern setting.

Colorado Historical Society
The Colorado Heritage Center
1300 Broadway
Denver, CO 80203
(303) 866-3682
● Plains Indian artifacts
specializing in those from
the people of the southern
and central plains. The fine
arts collection includes most
of the works and materials
from the studios of the western artists Charles Stobie and
Robert Lindneux, among
others.

Denver Art Museum
100 W. 14th Ave. Parkway
Denver, CO 80204
(303) 640-2295
● Approximately 15,000
American Indian objects
covering most tribal groups of
the United States and Canada.

Denver Museum of
Natural History
City Park
Denver, CO 80205
Mailing address:
2001 Colorado Blvd.
Denver, CO 80205
(303) 370-6357
● Native American Indian
collection.

Koshare Indian Museum
115 W. 18th St.
P.O. Box 580
La Junta, CO 81050
(719) 384-4411
● Indian baskets, beadwork,
and arts and crafts, as well as
over 400 paintings by Indian
and western artists.

ing to the American West and Southwest, as well as Native American art and artifacts.

The President Benjamin Harrison Home
1230 N. Delaware
Indianapolis, IN 46202
(317) 631-1898
● Collection housed in President Harrison's home includes political and campaign memorabilia as well as period furnishings (1874–1901).

William Hammond Mathers Museum
Indiana University
416 N. Indiana Ave.
Bloomington, IN 47405
Mailing address:
601 E. 8th St.
Bloomington, IN 47405
(812) 855-6873
● A museum of anthropology, history, and folklore. Included in its collections are some examples of Southwest Indian basketry, pots, and potsherds, rugs, and ceremonial artifacts.

IOWA
Effigy Mounds National Monument
R.R. 1, Box 25A
Harper's Ferry, IA 52146
(319) 873-3491
● The monument preserves a prehistoric Indian mound. The museum contains artifacts excavated from the mounds.

KANSAS
Last Indian Raid Museum
258 South Penn.
Oberlin, KS 67749
(913) 475-2712
● A museum based on West Kansas pioneers. General frontier artifacts with excellent Indian display.

Old Cowtown Museum
1871 Sim Park Drive
Wichita, KS 67203
(316) 264-0671
● A re-created early frontier village featuring 36 buildings that represent Wichita during the period of its early settlement and growth.

MAINE
Wilson Museum
Perkins St.
P.O. Box 196
Castine, ME 04421
(207) 326-8545
● Indian artifacts from California, Plains Indian beadwork, Pueblo pottery, fine western saddles collected before 1900.

MASSACHUSETTS
Peabody Museum of Archaeology and Ethnology
Harvard University
11 Divinity
Cambridge, MA 02138
(617) 495-2248
● The oldest museum in the nation devoted exclusively to the study of anthropology. It has some of the oldest and most complete native

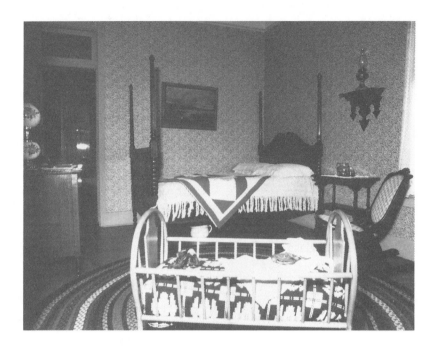

American collections in the world. All major cultural areas are represented; the Southwest, Northwest Coast, and Plains areas are the strongest.

MINNESOTA
Mille Lacs Indian Museum
Star Route Box 192
Onamia, MN 56359
(612) 532-3632
● Ojibway art and artifacts. Closed for renovations until 1995.

The Minnesota Historical Society
345 Kellogg Blvd. West
St. Paul, MN 55102-1906
(612) 296-6126
● Large collection of predominantly Sioux and Ojibway Indian artifacts. Some Southwest and Pacific Northwest Indian artifacts.

Pipestone National Monument
Box 727
Pipestone, MN 56164
(507) 825-5463
● Upper Plains Indian artifacts, primarily pipes and effigies carved from pipestone.

MISSOURI
Museum of Anthropology
104 Swallow Hall
University of Missouri
Columbia, MO 65211
(314) 882-3573
● Small collections of contemporary Southwest Indian jewelry and ceramics.

MONTANA

Yellowstone County Museum
Logan Field
Billings, MT 59101
Mailing address:
P.O. Box 959
Billings, MT 59103
(406) 256-6811
● Indian artifacts, antique collections of moccasins, western paintings, dioramas, old guns, and horse-drawn vehicles. Also a class L-7 steam locomotive.

NEBRASKA

Willa Cather Historical Center
338 North Webster St.
Red Cloud, NB 68970
Mailing address:
P.O. Box 326
Red Cloud, NB 68970
(402) 746-3285
● A branch museum of the Nebraska State Historical Society. The center properties include the Willa Cather Childhood Home restored and furnished to the period of Cather's residency as well as five other properties associated with Cather's life and writings. The center also maintains an archive of Cather books, manuscripts, documents, and photographs.

Museum of the Fur Trade
HC 74, Box 18
Chadron, NB 69337
(308) 432-3843
● Firearms, silverworks, textiles, cutlery, beads, and other trade artifacts, plus fine North American Indian items, trappers' equipment and early southwestern horse gear, weapons, and traveling outfits, all related to the North American fur trade.

NEW MEXICO

Acoma Tourist & Visitation Center
Corner of I-38 & I-23
P.O. Box 309
Pueblo of Acoma, NM 87034
(800) 747-0181
● Acoma, or "Sky City," is the oldest continuously inhabited city in the United States.

Albuquerque Museum
2000 Mountain Rd. N.W.
P.O. Box 1293
Albuquerque, NM 87103
(505) 243-7255
● Spanish Colonial artifacts from the 15th to the 19th century, territorial artifacts, western art with emphasis on New Mexico and the Southwest. Hispanic arts and crafts, limited collection of New Mexico native American materials, photoarchive with 45,000 images of Albuquerque from 1868 to the present.

Aztec Museum and Pioneer Village
125 N. Main
Aztec, NM 87410
(505) 334-9829
● Comprehensive exhibits of ancient (Anasazi) Indian artifacts and of Navajo Indian arts and crafts, four rooms of period furnishings, numerous indoor and outdoor exhibits of historic interest.

Aztec Ruins National Monument
Ruins Rd.
P.O. Box 640
Aztec, NM 87410
(505) 334-6174
● Museum and self-guiding trail explains life of the Anasazi Indians who lived here.

Blackwater Draw Museum
Rt. 70
Portales, NM 88130
Mailing address:
Eastern NM-Univ-Station 9
Portales, NM 88130
(505) 562-2202
● Collection of Indian artifacts.

Cimarron Historical Society
Hwy. 21, P.O. Box 58
Cimarron, NM 87714
(505) 376-2913
● History and artifacts of early Cimarron, the Santa Fe Trail, and the first settlers and ranchers of the area. Also, Ute and Jicarilla Apache artifacts.

Coronado State Monument
P.O. Box 95
State Hwy. 44
Bernalillo, NM 87004
(505) 867-5351
● The monument includes a walking tour through the ruins of a 14th-century pueblo, a visitors' center that houses original Pueblo painted murals, and a main exhibit room, which describes the life-styles of Pueblo Indians and Colonial Spanish peoples and their interactions.

Deming Luna Mimbres Museum
301 S. Silver
Deming, NM 88030
(505) 546-2382
● Indian artifacts, including Mimbres pottery, baskets, chuckwagon equipment, saddles and tack. Also a Quilt Room and a Doll Room.

Farmington Museum
302 North Orchard
Farmington, NM 87401
(505) 599-1179
● Material relevant to the social and cultural history of Farmington and the Four Corners area, which include Navajo, Hispanic, and Anglo cultures.

Grants Ceibola County Chamber of Commerce Museum
100 N. Iron St.
P.O. Box 297
Grants, NM 87020
(505) 287-4802

• Small museum with art, artifacts, pottery, mineral and basket collections from the area.

Governor Bent Museum
117 Bent St.
Taos, NM 87571
(505) 758-2376
• Western art featuring early Taos artists. Indian artifacts, baskets, pottery.

Indian Pueblo Cultural Center
2401 12th St. NW
Albuquerque, NM 87102
(505) 843-7270
• The center includes the Pueblo Indian Museum, which tells the story of the Pueblo Indians from prehistoric times to the present from the Indian point of view. Facilities also include Albuquerque's only native American restaurant and a gift shop featuring Indian handmade items.

Log Cabin Museum
33 Main St.
P.O. Box 83
Piños Altos, NM 88053
(505) 388-1882
• Indian artifacts from the area as well as articles connected with gold mining.

Los Alamos County Historical Museum
Fuller Lodge Cultural Center
1921 Juniper, P.O. Box 43
Los Alamos, NM 87544
(505) 662-4493
• A museum devoted to the history and culture of the Pajarito Plateau (Los Alamos).

Maxwell Museum of Anthropology
University of New Mexico
Albuquerque, NM 87131-1201
(505) 277-4404
• Archaeological and ethnographic collections of native North America with emphasis on the Southwest. The Dorothy and Gilbert Maxwell collection of southwestern weaving, mid-20th-century Hopi Kachinas, basketry (especially Northwest Coast), and Frances Newcomb sandpainting drawings.

Museum of International Folk Art
706 Camino Lejo
Santa Fe, NM 87501
Mailing address:
P.O. Box 2087
Santa Fe, NM 87504-2087
(505) 827-6350
• International collection of folk art including textiles, costumes, ceramics, dolls, and toys. Spanish Colonial religious art; Southwest Hispanic folk art and furniture; jewelry, amulets; religious and ceremonial and ritual objects.

Museum of New Mexico
113 Lincoln Ave.
Santa Fe, NM 87501
Mailing address:
Box 2087
Santa Fe, NM 87504-2087
• A museum of history, anthropology, fine arts, and folk art, with Indian,

Hispanic, and Anglo-American art and artifacts of southwestern origin. The Collection of Alexander Girard is also included.

The Old Coal Mine Museum
The Turquoise Trail
Hwy. 14
Madrid, NM 87010
(505) 473-0743
• Three acres of original buildings and displays of artifacts and equipment relating to the historic railroading and mining activities of the region.

Red Rock Museum
Red Rock State Park
P.O. Box 328
Church Rock, NM 87311
(505) 863-1337
• Exhibits of human and natural history of the Four Corners region.

Millicent Rogers Museum
P.O. Box A
Taos, NM 87571
(505) 758-2462
• An anthropology and art museum with collections of prehistoric and historic southwestern and Plains native American art and material culture; religious and secular arts of Hispanic New Mexico, the Maria Martinez (potter of San Ildefonso) family collection.

Roswell Museum and Art Center
100 W. 11th St.
Roswell, NM 88201
(505) 624-6744
● Municipal museum with collections specializing in art and artists of New Mexico. Southwestern painting, sculpture, and graphics, as well as extensive native American exhibits.

San Miguel Mission
401 Old Santa Fe Trail
Santa Fe, NM 87501
(505) 983-3974
● The original San Miguel Church was built circa 1610 and is today the oldest church still in active use in the United States. Inside the church are original skin paintings, statues, and other artworks dating from the 17th and 18th centuries.

Santuario de Nuestra Señora de Guadalupe
100 Guadalupe St.
Santa Fe, NM 87501
(505) 988-2027
● The Santuario is a "living" preservation, offering events in the fields of music, drama, art, education, and religion relevant to the history of the area. There are also exhibits of Spanish Colonial arts, Hispanic traditional and contemporary arts, and religious artifacts.

Silver City Museum
312 West Broadway
Silver City, NM 88061
(505) 538-5921
● Anthropological, archaeological, historical, and cultural collections, including Indian artifacts, household items of the early 20th century, ranching equipment, mining implements, photographs, legislative papers, and memorabilia.

Tularosa Basin Historical Society Museum
Box 518
1301 White Sand Blvd.
Alamogordo, NM 88310
(505) 437-4760
● A Pueblo pottery collection as well as a collection of the area's historical items, including a Chief Geronimo headdress.

Tularosa Village Historical Museum
501 Fresno
Tularosa, NM 88352
(505) 585-2057
● Collections representing the three cultures, Indian, Spanish/Mexican, and Anglo, concentrating on the Tularosa Village area.

The University Museum
New Mexico State University
Box 3564
University Avenue
Las Cruces, NM 88003
(505) 646-3739

● The museum's emphasis is on southwestern archaeology, ethnology, and history, especially of southern New Mexico and northern Mexico.

Western New Mexico University Museum
P.O. Box 680
Silver City, NM 88062
(505) 538-6386
● Anthropological, archaeological, historical, and cultural collections, including Indian artifacts, household items of the early 20th-century ranching equipment, mining implements, photographs, legislative papers, and memorabilia.

Wheelwright Museum of the American Indian
704 Camino Lejo
Santa Fe, NM 87501
Mailing address:
P.O. Box 5153
Santa Fe, NM 87502
(505) 982-4636

● The museum has three to four exhibits a year that feature both traditional and contemporary native American arts, crafts, and culture. The Case Trading Post and the museum shop offer a wide variety of native American arts and crafts for sale.

NEW YORK
American Museum of Natural History
Central Park West at 79th St.
New York, NY 10024
(212) 729-5000
● The Anthropology Department has extensive archaeological and ethnographic collections of North American Indian artifacts.

The Brooklyn Museum
200 Eastern Pkwy.
Box 1480
Brooklyn, NY 11283
(718) 638-5000

● Collections on native American cultures with special emphasis on the Southwest.

Museum of the American Indian
3753 Broadway at 155th St.
New York, NY 10032-1596
(212) 283-2420
● The museum is devoted to the collection, preservation, study, and exhibition of all things connected with the anthropology of the aboriginal peoples of North America and South America. Scheduled to move in November of 1994 to:
The Alexander Hamilton Custom House, 1 Bowling Green, New York, NY.
For further information, call:
(202) 357-3164

Ontario County Historical Society
55 N. Main St.
Canandaigua, NY 14424
(716) 394-4975
● Mary Clark Thompson collection of Southwest and Pacific Coast Indian baskets.

Rochester Museum & Science Center
657 East Ave.
Rochester, NY 14603-1480
(716) 271-4320
● Collections of Plains, Pueblo, Navajo, and

Northwest Coast Indian materials.

NORTH DAKOTA
Three Affiliated Tribes Museum
P.O. Box 836
New Town, ND 58763
(701) 627-4477
● The museum houses a large library and collections representing the heritage and culture of the tribes that inhabited and still inhabit the area.

OKLAHOMA
Ataloa Lodge Museum
Bacone College
2299 Old Bacone Rd.
Muskogee, OK 74403-1597
(918) 683-4581
● Collections of spears, arrowheads, Navajo rugs, pottery, and baskets.

Creek Council House Museum
Town Square
Okmulgee, OK 74447
(918) 756-2324
● A National Historic Landmark dedicated to the preservation and collection of all materials relating to the Muskogee Creek tribe.

The Five Civilized Tribes Museum
Agency Hill
Honor Heights Drive
Muskogee, OK 74401
(918) 683-1701
● The story of the Five Civilized Tribes, Cherokee, Choctaw, Chickasaw, Creek, and Seminole is told through art, artifacts, and books.

Thomas Gilcrease Institute of American History and Art
1400 Gilcrease Museum Rd.
Tulsa, OK 74127
(918) 582-3122

● Art, artifacts, books, and documents relating to the growth and development of America.

The National Hall of Fame for Famous American Indians
Hwy. 62 East of Anadarko
P.O. Box 548
Anadarko, OK 73005
(405) 247-5555
(405) 247-3331
● A shrine dedicated to American Indians who have helped shape the American culture.

Oklahoma Museum of Natural History
University of Oklahoma
1335 Asp Ave.
Norman, OK 73109
(405) 325-4711
● Collections pertaining to native American ethnology and archaeology.

Pawnee Bill Museum
Box 493
Pawnee, OK 74058
(918) 762-2513
● Museum and home of the late Gordon W. Lillie, known as Pawnee Bill.

State Museum of History
2100 N. Lincoln Blvd.
Oklahoma City, OK 73105
(405) 521-2491
● Exhibits and research collections related to Oklahoma history and prehistory.

Woolaroc Museum
Rt. 3, State Hwy. #123
Bartlesville, OK 74003
(918) 336-0307
● Western and southwestern art, native American art and artifacts, material relating to cowboys and pioneers, and Colt weapons.

OREGON

Marion County Historical Society
260 12th St., S.E.
Salem, OR 97301-4101
(503) 364-2128
● A collection of Kalapuyian Indian artifacts, including a canoe and basketry.

Ox Barn Museum
Second and Liberty Streets
P.O. Box 202
Aurora, OR 97002
(503) 678-5754
● Artifacts from the Aurora Colony, a German religious communal society that settled at Aurora, Oregon, from 1856 to 1883.

Portland Art Museum
1219 S.W. Park
Portland, OR 97205
(503) 226-2811
● Indian and western art and artifacts. Works by artists from Oregon and the Northwest. Southwest Indian baskets and pottery.

RHODE ISLAND

Tomaquag Indian Memorial Museum
Summit Rd.
Exeter, RI 02822
(401) 539-7213
● Small collections of southwestern pottery and basketry, some material from the Basin, Plains, and Northwest Coast Indians.

SOUTH DAKOTA

W. H. Over State Museum
University of South Dakota
1110 Ratingen
Vermillion, SD 57069
Mailing address:
414 E. Clark
Vermillion, SD 57069
(605) 677-5228
● The David and Elizabeth Clark Memorial Collection of Plains Indians artifacts and the Stanley J. Morrow Historic Photograph Collection of the Dakota territory and area.

TEXAS

LBJ State Park
P.O. Box 238
Stonewall, TX 78671
(210) 644-2252
● Small museums of gifts received by the President. Tours of ranch available. Living history farm.

Texas Memorial Museum
2400 Trinity
Austin, TX 78705
(512) 471-1604
● Collections include ethnographic artifacts from North American Plains and south-western Indians, as well as extensive collections of cattle-ranching-related items, historic firearms, Texas history, and photographs.

University of Texas at Austin
Winedale Historical Center
FM Road 2714
P.O. Box 11
Round Top, TX 78954
(409) 278-3530
● Center for the study of the ethnic cultures of Central Texas, consisting of a 190-acre farmstead with original house and outbuildings and three additional pre–Civil War buildings.

WASHINGTON

Thomas Burke Memorial Washington State Museum
University of Washington
Seattle, WA 98195
(206) 543-5590
● The natural-history museum of the state of Washington, with an important collection of native American material, particularly that of the Columbia Plateau and the Northwest Coast.

Fort Okanogan
Interpretive Center
Alta Lake State Park
HCR 88, Box 40
Pateros, WA 98846
(509) 923-2473
● Collections of Indian and western artifacts circa 1830–1870.

Fort Vancouver National Historic Site
1501 E. Evergreen Blvd.
Vancouver, WA 98661
(206) 696-7655
● The largest collection of Hudson's Bay Company fur trade artifacts in North America.

Makah Cultural and Research Center
P.O. Box 95
Neah Bay, WA 98357
(206) 645-2711
● The Makah Museum is owned and operated by the Makah Indian Nation and houses, preserves, and displays the more than 55,000 artifacts discovered at the Ozette archaeological site 15 miles south of Neah Bay.

WISCONSIN

Logan Museum of
Anthropology
700 College St.
Beloit, WI 53511
(608) 363-2677
● Southwestern, Northern
Plains, and Great Lakes
American Indian collections.

Milwaukee Public Museum
800 W. Wells St.
Milwaukee, WI 53233
(414) 278-2702
● A large collection of North
American Indian artifacts.

WYOMING

Bradford Brinton Memorial
239 Brinton Rd.
Box 460
Bighorn, WY 82833
(307) 672-3173
● Indian items collected by
Mr. Brinton, including baskets, rugs, blankets, and
clothing.

Buffalo Bill Historical Center
720 Sheridan Ave.
P.O. Box 1000
Cody, WY 82414
(307) 587-4771
● One of the world's most
complete collections of western artifacts, art, and memorabilia, including the Plains
Indian Museum, Whitney
Gallery of Western Art,
Winchester Arms Museum,
and Buffalo Bill Museum.

Fort Bridger State Museum
P.O. Box 35
Fort Bridger, WY 82933
(307) 787-6795
● Northern Plains tribes artifacts, military equipment,
western Americana, Mountain
Men–era materials, and
women's apparel.

Fort Casper Museum
4001 Fort Casper Rd.
Casper, WY 82604
(307) 235-8462
● Plains Indians beadwork
and Indian artifacts from
1860 to 1930. Also many
western materials associated
with Fort Caspar and central
Wyoming.

Fort Laramie National
Historic Site
Box 86
Fort Laramie, WY 82212
(307) 837-2221
● A 19th-century military
post with seven furnished his-
toric house museums depict-

ing military and civilian life,
with Northern Plains and
Southwestern Plains Indian
tribes represented.

Laramie Plains Museum
603 Ivinson Ave.
Laramie, WY 82070-3299
(307) 742-4448
● A historical museum
housed in a Victorian mansion. Collections deal primarily with the history of the
Laramie Plains area and
people.

Wyoming State Museum
Barrett Building
2301 Central Ave.
Cheyenne, WY 82002
(307) 777-7022
● The museum maintains
and exhibits a collection of
prehistoric, historic, and fine-
arts objects related to the
development of Wyoming
and the American West.
Collections include Plains
Indian material, historic textiles and clothing, military
artifacts, furniture, paintings,
drawings, prints, sculptures,
and household and personal
equipment.

275

Index

A

Adobe houses, 32–33, 36–83
  granite imitation of, 78–83
  haciendas, 58–63, 68–73
  Oriental details in, 74–77
  studios, 36–41, 55–56
  technique of, 39
American Country West style, 7–9
Anasazi Indians, 11
Animals. *See also* Bison
  afterlife of, 16–17
  drawings of, 70–71
  pelts of, 113, 116–17, 120–21
Antlers, 16–17, 117
Apache heritage, 39–41
Arbors, 16–17
Arches, 98
Archways, 16–17
Armijo, Federico, 79
Austin, Bill, 191

B

Baker, Nancy, 191
Barns, 6–7, 16–17, 101
Baskets, 44–45, 72, 109, 117, 139, 177, 185, 210–11
  Apache "circus," 44–45
  Tlingit, 110
Bathrooms, 87, 140–41
Beacon Mills, 179, 180
Beaded novelties, 51
Beadwork, 109
Beams, 51, 54–56, 67, 97, 115, 132–33
  vigas, 55–56, 67, 69
Beaudet, Dean, 230–31
Becket, MacDonald, 102–5
Bedposts, 190–91, 222–23, 231
Bedrooms
  farmhouse, 152–55, 162–63
  in log houses, 90–91, 97, 100–101, 117
  master, 192–93
Beds, 122, 143, 145, 185, 222–23, 231, 239. *See also* Daybeds; Headboards
  African, 76
  four-poster, 111, 154–55, 162–63
  Fredericksburg, 90–91
  rolling pin, 91
  scallop-trimmed, 153
  spindle, 112
  spool, 152–53
Bell, Bill, 203
Belts, 203, 204–5

Benches, 63, 76, 108, 113, 131, 136–37, 164, 227, 237
Bettis, Pop, 199
Birdhouses, 125
Birds, wooden, 164
Birrittella, Buffy, 175–77
Bison, 128–29, 252–53
Blanco, Teodora, 75
Blankets, 128–29, 179–80, 183
  Navajo, 43, 56, 174–75
  saddle, 105, 109
Blinds, window, 79
Bookcases, 97, 110
Boulders, 78–79, 81
Branding irons, 189, 196–97, 199
Broholm, Dale, 83
Bronze casting, 208–9
Brooks, Winn, 125
Brown, William Ernest, 133
Brumder, Nick, 98
Buffalo Bill Historical Center, 240–43
Bush, Nan, 179, 180

C

Cabinets, 57, 83, 91, 96, 99, 150
Cactus, 74–75, 79, 81
Cappellucci, Chris, 95
Cappellucci, Steve, 93–101, 226–29
Carey, Ryan, 214
Carter, Charles, 237
Casa San Ysidro, 58–63
Casso, copper, 60–61
Caywood, Robert and Jackie, 108–9
Ceilings, 59
Ceramics. *See* Pottery
Chairbacks, 224
Chairs, 89, 99, 128, 130–31, 150–51, 224–25, 239
  barrel, 131
  booted, 131
  Cappellucci, 228–29
  high, 228–29
  high-backed, 222-23
  Kentucky weaver's, 161
  Kentucky willow, 112
  ladder-back, 105
  lodgepole pine, 230
  mule deer, 168–69
  natural bentwood, 130
  pony decaled, 122–23
  rocking, 122, 224–25, 228–29
  twig, 143, 172–73, 175
  windsor, 175
Chandeliers, 99, 190–91
"Checks," 230–31
Chests, 51, 60, 63, 81, 111, 112

Chimayo weavings, 199, 216–19, 222–23
Churches, 28–29
Cigar store Indian, 53
Cochran, Robbie and Lee, 149–53
Cody, William F. (Buffalo Bill), 240–43
Coin bank, 77
Colter, John, 248–49
Conchas, 203
Corbels, 59, 67, 71
Courtyards, 70–71, 134
Cowboys
  clothing and equipment of, 1–3
  as craftsmen, 9, 196–209
  as folk heroes, 7, 8
  rodeo, 244–47
Cross, inlaid, 76
Cupboards, 99, 158, 160, 162–63, 164–65
Cups, leather, 200

D

Davis, Dave, 164
Daybeds, 122–23, 149, 155
Decks, 94, 138–39
Dining rooms, 47, 82–83, 99, 150–51, 160–61, 168–69
Dolls, 44, 45, 72, 109, 111
Dominick, Marshall, 122
Doors, 34–36, 39, 69, 79, 239
Dormers, 251
Dresses, 104–5, 211
Drummond, Sir William, 121
Dwellings, Indian, 7, 10–11

E

Edgar, Bob, 3, 234–37
Edgar, Terry, 3, 235–37
Emmerling, Mary, 101
Empie, Bill, 79
Empie, Sunnie, 79, 81

F

Fachwerk style, 33, 88, 91
Fannie Bell rockers, 224–25
Farmhouses, 32–33, 146–71
Fashions, Santa Fe, 177
Fay, Clint, 205
Fences, 30–31, 57
Fireplaces, 51, 82–83, 88, 109, 110, 126–27. *See also* Hearths
  iron hood of, 138–39

stone-and-timber, 104
Fishing, 248
Flag, centennial, 132–33
Floors, painted, 190–91
Food warmers, 158
Frescoes, 43–44, 46–47, 70–71
Frontier towns, 18–19
Furniture making, 220–31
  Colorado rustic style of, 226–29
  Idaho rustic style of, 230–31
  ranch style of, 220–23
  Spanish New Mexican style of, 224–25

G

Gateways, 30
Gimme cap collection, 26–27
Giraffes, folk-art, 52–53
Girard, Alexander and Susan, 75
Glomb, Skip, 208–9
Gould, Peter, 224–25
Green, Austin (Slim), 3, 42–43, 196–201
Grinding stones, 69
Guest houses, 93, 98–100, 121, 180

H

Haciendas, 58–63, 68–73
Hall tree, Texas, 169
Harinero, 63
Harrison, Benjamin, 1
Harrison, William Henry, 1
Hat racks, 164
Hay, newly rolled, 14–15
Headboards, 91, 97, 100
Headdress, feather, 104
Hearths, 47, 60–61, 72–73, 94, 97, 110, 111, 189
Hindman, Paul, 220, 221
Hoback, Priscilla, 56, 212–15, 224
Hogg, Ima, 164
Holsters, 205
Hopper, Melody, 222–23
Hopper, Stan, 220–23
Horses, carved, 55, 187
Horticulture, 13, 57, 74–75
Horwitch, Elaine, 43–53
House of Clouds, 64–67
Houses, 7, 32–171
  adobe, 32–33, 36–83
  custom kit, 103, 114–15, 194
  farmhouses, 32–33, 146–71
  log, 84–117
  ornamental, 77
Hysong, Andy, 202

I

ndians. *See* Native Americans; *and individual tribes*
ron pieces, 67

J

erga, 60
ohnson, Charles Foreman, 79
ohnson, Lady Bird, 166–71
ohnson, Lyndon Baines, Ranch, 166
osoff, Jim, 133–35

K

Kelter-Malce, 180
King, Don, 207
Kitchens, 48–50, 56–57, 96, 110, 139, 150, 158–59, 176–77, 184, 238–39
Kiva, 65
Knife, swivel, 205

L

Ladders, 89, 90–91
La Fontaine, Glen, 81
Lamp base, 229
Lamps, 144
Lampshades, 127–28, 144
Lanterns, 159, 194–95, 197
Lariats, 207
Larom, Larry, 125, 127
Latillas, 56, 67
Lauren, Ralph, 175, 177
Leather tooling, 204–5
Lintels, window, 99
Living rooms, 42–43, 44, 77, 97
  Art Deco, 142–43
  farmhouse, 149, 169
  ranch house, 139, 145
Lofts, sleeping, 41, 89
Log houses, 84–117
  in the East, 186–95
  German influence on, 86–91
  handcrafted, 92–101
  miniatures, 194–95
Looms, 216–19
Love seats, 99
Luevand, A. V., 1–3
Lyndon Baines Johnson Ranch, 166–71

M

McLaughlin, Jim and "Buckskin" Jenny, 125
McLean, Mac, 214
Magleby, Frank, 112
Main streets, 18–19
Malce, Michael, 180
Mead, Chris, 183
Mesa dwellings, 11
Messer, Tom, 157–64
Heyer pottery, 150, 158
Middleton, James, 164
Minges, Alan and Shirley, 59–63
Miniature, Pueblo, 77
Mirrors, 140–41
Mojave ceramics, 44, 47
Molesworth, Thomas, 127, 128, 220
Monument Valley, 10–11
Mountain men, 20–23
Mullins, Barry, 164
Murphy, Rosalea, 55

N

Nameplate, 191
Napkins, bandanna, 184
Native Americans. *See also individual tribes*
  cultural contributions of, 1, 8–9
Navajo blankets, 43, 56, 174–75
Navajo rugs, 60–61, 81, 111, 120–21, 128–29, 175
Navajo weavings, 8–9, 105, 107
Nieto, John, 36–41, 189

O

Old Faithful geyser, 249
Old Faithful Inn, 250–51
Old Trail Town, 232–33, 235–37
Ollas, 81
Ortega, David, 216–17
Oviedo, Marco, 219

P

Paintings, 56, 164, 188–89
  fresco, 43–44, 46–47
"Pancho," 53
Pantry, 96
Papago pottery, 81
Patterns, geometric, 8–9
Pendleton Mills, 175, 179
Peralta-Ramos, Arturo, 71–72
Pie safes, 148–49, 164–65
Pio Pico mansion, 239
Pit houses, 11
Plains Indian Museum, 241
Porches, 95, 140, 187, 194–95
Portraits, bronze, 209
Pots, 50, 93, 111, 132–33, 134, 177
Pottery, 44–45, 109, 212–15
  Meyer, 150, 158
  Mojave, 44, 47
  original plaster, 214–15
  painted glazes on, 213
  Papago, 81
Pottinger, Fred, 157–64
Pueblo Indians, 11, 19, 69
Pueblos, 18–19

Q

Quilts, 112, 153–55, 171, 192–93

R

Racks, 177
Ramos, Jackie, 71–72
Ranch houses, 118–45
Reamer, Robert C., 251
Remington, Frederic, 241–42
Reynolds, Nancy Clark, 187–95
Riddle, Dewey and Elsie, 121
Robinson Bar Ranch, 189
Rodeos, 244–47
Rogers, Millicent, 69–71
Roofs, 6–7, 56, 99, 108, 125, 133, 239
Ropemaking, 199, 206–7
Rowels, 202
Rugs, 60–61, 73, 112, 145
  braided, 153
  hooked, 155
  Navajo, 60–61, 81, 111, 120–21, 128–29, 175
Ryman, John, 180

S

Saddles, 42–43, 198–202
Salazar, Leo, 111
Saloons, 24–27
Santa Fe Indian Market, 211
School houses, 236–37
Sculpture, 75, 81, 214–15, 242
"Semi Dazzler," 105, 107
Seven D Ranch, 118–23
Silverwork, 199, 203
Sims, Agnes, 56
Sinks
  Art Nouveau, 140–41
  dry, 177
Skins, 16–17
Skulls, 16–17, 65, 87, 103, 110
Sloane, Eric, 65
Sloane, Mimi, 67
Smokey the Bear, 249
Snowshoes, 116–17, 122
Sofas, 113, 162, 185, 222–23
Spas, 106–7
"Spirit hole," 36, 39, 41
Spurs, 110, 202
Stedes, Patsy, 171
Stirrups, 66, 194–95
Stoneware, 57, 139
Stools, 76, 83, 95, 224
Storytelling, 73, 107
Stoves, 59
Swazo, Joseph, 71

T

Tables, 81, 89, 105, 159, 162
gator-legged, 145
Mexican, 50
Molesworth, 222–23
pine, 48–49, 188–89
redwood, 134
sawbuck, 175
Tackmaking, 202
Texas star, 166
Thorne, Oakleigh, II, 127
Trastero, Mexican, 83
Troughs, 66, 95, 99, 101
Trujillo, Irvin, 218–19
Trujillo, Isabelle, 219
Trujillo, Jacobo, 219

U

Uncle Sam, 53

V

Valentine, Western, 6–7
Valley Ranch, 125–27
Vigas, 55–56, 67, 69

W

Wagons, 189, 195, 232–33, 235
Wagon wheels, 110, 117, 235
Walls
  adobe, 43, 60, 72
  chinked log, 105
  horseshoe-shaped, 40–41
  limestone, 171
  mortar-free, 157
  shipwreck-salvaged, 180–81
  solar, 39
Weavings, 72
  Chimayo, 199, 216–19, 222–23
  Navajo, 8–9, 105, 107
Weber, Bruce, 179
Weigl, Lee, 171
West, the
  colors and textures of, 12–15
  in the East, 172–95
  heritage of, 232–54
  settlement of, 7
White, Roy, 171
Whitney, Gloria Vanderbilt, 241–42
Winchester Arms Museum, 241
Window boxes, 93
Windows, 99, 113, 179
Woletto Indian art, 51
Work, David, 95, 227, 228
Workshops, 224–25, 226–27
Wreaths, 190–91, 197
Wyoming Furniture Company, 220–23

Y

Yellowstone National Park, 248–51

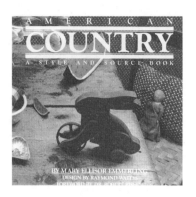

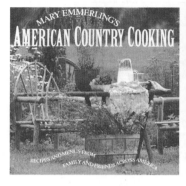

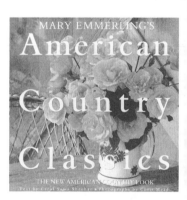

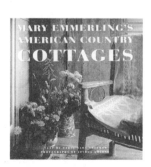
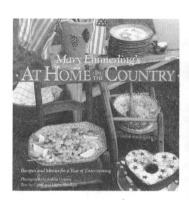